W9-CFG-164

by Blake Busick and Christie Latona

with The California-Nevada Annual Conference

FOREWORD BY PAUL NIXON

Catch Fire in 50 days

Joining the Movement of God's Mission in the World

Readiness 360 Edition

Imagine what would happen if more than half of those who attend worship actually joined the movement of God's mission in the world....

 How would we be different?

 How would people's lives—inside and outside the church—be changed?

 How would our mission to make disciples of Jesus Christ for the transformation of the world be experienced & enhanced?

 What might be indications that we had become a movement again?

We must give ourselves away so that God might use us to be God's agents of transformation in our churches and communities. We pray that enough **people** catch on fire that God's love and grace might set the world on Holy Spirit fire—and that we Easter people might have Pentecost experiences regularly.

This 50-day study grew out of the work of a diverse group of people from the California-Nevada Annual Conference of the United Methodist Church. They sought to discern how to encourage and support the development of vital faith communities across their region in a way which would be pleasing to God. This group includes:

Bishop Warner Brown, Blake Busick, Carolyn Talmadge, Christie Latona (consultant), Donald Guest, Gabriela Perla, Maria Perla, George Bennett, Kelly Deditius, Kris Marshall, Kristin Stoneking, Linda Caldwell, Maile Koloto, Marcelo Escarzaga, Ron Dunn, and Sung-Ho Lee.

Even though the group conceived the idea of the study, the birthing was accomplished primarily through Blake Busick.

Please share your reflections, responses and questions on
www.facebook.com/catchfirein50
www.catchfirein50days.com

Cover and Book Design by Bill Kersey, KerseyGraphics

Table of Contents

Foreword

"Fire!"

You can get arrested just for the shouting of that word in certain places. Fire is dangerous, wild, unpredictable, difficult to order and control, a crazy thing. It is also mesmerizing.

When I was a kid I would sit in front of our fireplace for hours and watch the fire dancing, crackling and leaping. During that same early season of my life I also was blessed to come to my own faith in Christ as part of a California congregation that caught *Spirit Fire*! I experienced my call to ministry there. My whole life and work has been a response to that Fire. Three new faith communities planted years later, each more than 2000 miles away, each are directly in response to what began in that 1970s Fire that swept our church, which was itself directly in response to earlier Fires, tracing their way back to Pentecost!

In the late 70s, our family moved back east, leaving that congregation behind. Across the years, I gave thanks for that magical season of my own spiritual birth, and the quadrupling of our church in about three years' time. It was the music of that time and place that I most remembered, and the baptisms. All ages, hundreds of them, baptized, filled with God's joy, their lives transformed. My dad used to tell me that when I was an old man with a long white beard I would still be talking about that time. I assumed that I would never see it again. That lightning surely would not strike twice. I had just been lucky.

Then 20 years later, in an upstairs room at a restaurant in northwest Florida, on a day when I least expected it, the Fire came again. Eight of us gathered in that room for a lunch meeting, each confused about our church's future. Two hours later, we left full of the Spirit and ready to immediately buy 13 acres of land. Hundreds of new people came into that church in the wake of that Firey lunch encounter in that upper room. From that day on, I knew that Fire is not intended to be the exception, but the norm. In fact, nothing much of value in the Christian movement has ever happened except in response to the Fire of God.

New Spirit energy continues to grow new ministries, to draw diverse people and to create a church that mirrors heaven a little more each week. As with any fire, you cannot understand it from afar! You have to be there. You can't do Pentecost at a distance, or just by studying Acts 2 or reading about Wesley or Azura Street. Pentecost finally has to happen anew. It has to happen to you and to the people you call church. It just has to!

We can make our strategic plans and run our capital campaigns until the cows come home, and it won't amount to much in the end. Unless the Fire comes.

This 50-day adventure is about waiting for God's Fire, anticipating it, longing for it, and then receiving it with joy and wonderment! It is not an adventure for the faint of heart.

Fire will rock your world. And forever change it.

Paul Nixon
Ministry coach, speaker and author of
We Refused to Lead a Dying Church
and other books on church transformation.
Co-developer, Readiness 360

An Invitation

Warning! For the next 50 days you are invited to immerse yourself in the story of the church becoming a movement of grace transforming the world. What you are about to read is very dangerous, even disruptive. It is the story of the power of Christ's resurrection set loose in the world through the fire of the Holy Spirit. It is a story that is:

- Dangerous to systems that perpetuate crushing poverty and poor health.
- Disruptive to a world bent on violence and war.
- Deadly to the forces that keep people lost, addicted, hopeless, oppressed or ignorant of the fact that they are children of God.

At its core, it is a love story. It reveals to us that we live in a world that God so loves, and that God will stop at nothing to express the Creator's grace, mercy, compassion and justice to that world. You are a part of this story. You belong to a church and to an extended family of believers. Together we give expression to this love story by making disciples of Jesus Christ who transform the world by their new life in Christ.

We are approaching the dawn of a new day among our churches and people. It is a day that will not be birthed by our plans and strategies and efforts, but by the gracious work of the Holy Spirit. Our work is a loving response to what God is doing in our midst. **Catch Fire in 50 Days** is an opportunity for us to pray and prepare for that new day when we as a Church become a movement again.

If we need to, let's repent of church as we want it to be. Let's repent of small thinking and puny visions. Let's repent of self-absorption and viewing church as something we consume.

Let's turn toward God's vision and God's world and the call of Christ to get about God's mission. It is not about trying to save or maintain our local church. It is about losing our lives in God's mission, knowing that as we lose our lives in Christ we will find them again. It is about God's mission to bring good news to the poor, release to the captives, recovery of sight to the blind; to set at liberty those who are oppressed and to proclaim the year of God's favor. If we are just trying to hang on to our lives, our churches, we will lose them.

The world needs churches to be vital today, more vital tomorrow and even more vital the day after. It is not about us. It is about God and the world God so loves.

Let's catch fire as we open ourselves to God through these daily Scripture readings. Let's pray that God would make us a movement again. It can start with a single heart igniting through a fresh encounter with Christ. *Could that heart be yours?*

Using this Guide

After witnessing the resurrected Christ, the apostles were sent to be his witnesses to the ends of the earth. Through the power of the Holy Spirit, the first disciples of Jesus became a movement that transformed the world. The beginning of their story is told in the Book of Acts. It continues through Jesus' followers today!

The core of this guide is centered in the first 13 chapters in the book of Acts. If you are using this in conjunction with a preaching series, we encourage you to start the 50 days on a Sunday. With the exception of the first week, every Monday through Friday is an immersion in the unfolding drama of the early Christian movement as described in **Acts**. Every Sunday is a **Gospel** reading. Most Saturdays offer an encounter with **First Peter**.

The Gospel readings offer an opportunity to have a fresh encounter with Jesus. It is this encounter which can (re)ignite a Holy Spirit fire within you. It is this fire that is the energy of the movement we seek to become. The readings from Acts show us how the fire which spread so rapidly 2,000 years ago can do so again in our time. The passages from First Peter provide encouragement to sustain that fire in the midst of difficult, troubling times.

Each day you are asked to **Read** the assigned passage; **Reflect** on what you have read; and **Respond** in faith. Questions for reflection and a response to consider are suggested each day. These are only suggestions. You may have better questions to ponder and a different response to make.

In the book, we have included contributions from persons who did this study from Easter to Pentecost 2011, as extra encouragement for your own reflection. The key to this journey is to read a little, reflect a little, and pray a little (or a lot) each day. It will not be the same to try to cram all the reading in a weekend. Use the full 50 days! At some point along the journey, whether in private reading time, in service to others or at a time gathered with your church, you should expect that the Holy Spirit will begin to stir in you and to prompt you to certain actions. We encourage you to take good notes as this happens, to share what you are hearing with your closest colleagues in faith and to respond thoughtfully and faithfully.

We are an Easter people. The resurrection of Jesus from the dead is the spark for everything else. Therefore for the entire first week, you will be immersed in the resurrection story as told by the four gospels, the preaching of Peter and the writing of Paul. After this first week the pattern as outlined above will be followed.

Pray that we might have a fresh encounter with Jesus; that the power of Christ's resurrection might again be set loose in the world through the fire of the Holy Spirit within us. Pray that this season of prayer and reflection might have a lasting impact on our congregations and communities.

Let's set the world on fire!

Additional Resources

Small Group Template

Use the template found at the end of this guide to align your small groups with this daily devotional. You may want to start new short-term small groups in order to have a church-wide study using this guide as the curriculum for 50 days.

Sermon Outlines & Multimedia Support

We have slides and sermon outlines that enable this guide to be used to support a 50-day spiritual campaign in which the Sunday message, daily devotions and small group discussions are all aligned. Pastors may choose to use the Saturday text (First Peter) or the Sunday text (lectionary Gospel for the day) as the basis for the preached word.

Catch Fire e-devotionals

Whenever you start your 50 days, you can sign up at **catchfirein50days.net/e-fire** to receive daily emails to help keep you on track.

Facebook Community

Need we say more? Interact with others on the journey. Share insights, struggles and questions. Post prayers. **www.facebook.com/catchfirein50**.

Readiness 360

If your congregation hasn't already taken the Readiness 360 survey and viewed the report, you will want to add this very important step to your discernment process. Learn more at **www.readiness360.org/tools/catch-fire/**.

Week 1

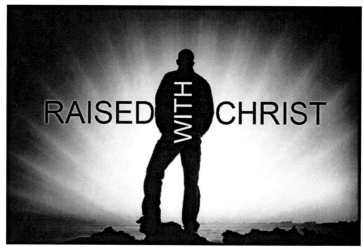

RAISED WITH CHRIST

In order to become a movement of God's mission in the world we must BE who are, SEE what we have and DO what matters to God.* This simple transformational process forms a basis for our study and helps congregations realign themselves with God's vision for them in the world.

God has blessed us with a rich diversity of spiritual sisters and brothers around the world. Each of us, therefore, will embody this process uniquely in our context. But our uniqueness draws from a common source and identity. We are an Easter people! However we describe ourselves (BE); however we identify the resources we individually and collectively have (SEE); Or however we act in mission (DO); it all originates in the resurrection of Jesus Christ.

Immerse yourself this week in the stories of Christ's resurrection and significance. Experience anew what it means to be raised with Christ (Colossians 3:1). Get (re)engaged in daily practices that will rekindle your spiritual intensity.

BE who you are ≫ SEE what you have ≫ DO what matters to God

*Model developed by A Renewal Enterprise (http://www.arenewalenterprise.com/)

You know well enough how the wind blows this way and that. You hear it rustling through the trees, but you have no idea where it comes from or where it's headed next. That's the way it is with everyone 'born from above' by the wind of God, the Spirit of God.

Jesus,
John 3:8, *The Message*

Catch Fire in 50 Days

Pray for guidance and discernment. If you wish, write that prayer here and use it for the next six days.

Read John 20:1–18 slowly and prayerfully. What words or phrases stand out for you?

Early on the first day of the week, while it was still dark, Mary Magdalene came to the tomb and saw that the stone had been removed from the tomb. ²So she ran and went to Simon Peter and the other disciple, the one whom Jesus loved, and said to them, "They have taken the Lord out of the tomb, and we do not know where they have laid him." ³Then Peter and the other disciple set out and went toward the tomb. ⁴The two were running together, but the other disciple outran Peter and reached the tomb first. ⁵He bent down to look in and saw the linen wrappings lying there, but he did not go in. ⁶Then Simon Peter came, following him, and went into the tomb. He saw the linen wrappings lying there, ⁷and the cloth that had been on Jesus' head, not lying with the linen wrappings but rolled up in a place by itself. ⁸Then the other disciple, who reached the tomb first, also went in, and he saw and believed; ⁹for as yet they did not understand the scripture, that he must rise from the dead. ¹⁰Then the disciples returned to their homes.

¹¹But Mary stood weeping outside the tomb. As she wept, she bent over to look into the tomb; ¹²and she saw two angels in white, sitting where the body of Jesus had been lying, one at the head and the other at the feet. ¹³They said to her, "Woman, why are you weeping?" She said to them, "They have taken away my Lord, and I do not know where they have laid him." ¹⁴When she had said this, she turned around and saw Jesus standing there, but she did not know that it was Jesus. ¹⁵Jesus said to her, "Woman, why are you weeping? Whom are you looking for?" Supposing him to be the gardener, she said to him, "Sir, if you have carried him away, tell me where you have laid him, and I will take him away." ¹⁶Jesus said to her, "Mary!" She turned and said to him in Hebrew, "Rabbouni!" (which means Teacher). ¹⁷Jesus said to her, "Do not hold on to me, because I have not yet ascended to the Father. But go to my brothers and say to them, 'I am ascending to my Father and your Father, to my God and your God.'" ¹⁸Mary

Magdalene went and announced to the disciples, "I have seen the Lord"; and she told them that he had said these things to her.

Reflect

What is the significance of this story to you personally? To your local church? To the body of believers?

With whom do you identify most in the story? Peter? The other disciple? Mary? One of the disciples who received Mary's witness?

Respond

Considering that we are an Easter people, do one thing differently or more boldly today because of the resurrection of Jesus Christ.

Encouragement: *You Are Known*

> My greatest need is to be known; to be known for who I truly am — not just by the multitude of personas I wear, but by my true self, unmasked.
>
> My greatest fear is to be known; for who could bear my true self? Who would not be horrified or repelled by the true Blake, exposed?
>
> I heard my name today spoken by One I thought was a stranger, but now I see was my Lord. He called my name. I am fully known and yet He did not abandon me but rather raised me with Him.
>
> I think I just caught fire!
>
> *Blake Busick*

Pray that you and all who participate in these 50 days of reading, reflecting and response will hear their name called by Christ and encounter Him in powerful and transforming ways so that we all might acknowledge that we are raised with Christ.

Begin with the prayer for guidance and discernment you wrote on Day 1.

Read Matthew 28:1–10 slowly and prayerfully. What words or phrases stand out for you?

> *After the Sabbath, as the first day of the week was dawning, Mary Magdalene and the other Mary went to see the tomb. ²And suddenly there was a great earthquake; for an angel of the Lord, descending from heaven, came and rolled back the stone and sat on it. ³His appearance was like lightning, and his clothing white as snow. ⁴For fear of him the guards shook and became like dead men. ⁵But the angel said to the women, "Do not be afraid; I know that you are looking for Jesus who was crucified. ⁶He is not here; for he has been raised, as he said. Come, see the place where he lay. ⁷Then go quickly and tell his disciples, 'He has been raised from the dead, and indeed he is going ahead of you to Galilee; there you will see him.' This is my message for you." ⁸So they left the tomb quickly with fear and great joy, and ran to tell his disciples. ⁹Suddenly Jesus met them and said, "Greetings!" And they came to him, took hold of his feet, and worshiped him. ¹⁰Then Jesus said to them, "Do not be afraid; go and tell my brothers to go to Galilee; there they will see me."*

Reflect

Where are you looking for Jesus?

What would you have to let go of in order to allow for an unexpected in-breaking of Christ in your life?

Who do you know who needs to hear this message of Christ's resurrection? In what way can you share it with them by word or by deed?

Respond

In the name of Jesus, tell one person to not be afraid.

Encouragement: *Fear? Step Out Anyway*

Fear. One small four-letter word that seems to be so powerful. Read our lesson today: the guards "for fear of him"; the angel to the woman, "do not be afraid"; the disciples, "for they left the tomb with fear and great joy." Then Jesus said to them, "Do not be afraid."

That word fear seems to permeate our world today, as well. If you doubt that, watch the nightly news or pick up a newspaper or surf the Internet. Fear is pervasive. In the Church, we have used fear as well, often as a cautionary tale of why the Church should not attempt some new or innovative approach to ministry. Ordained clergy have called it the seven words, "We've never done it that way before." Utter that phrase at a Church Council meeting or an Annual Conference Session and one can feel the tension of fear. And then in fear, we step back from the opportunity: Better to be safe than sorry, we rationalize.

Jesus understood that. Jesus understands that. Spoken first by the angels and later by Jesus, "Do not be afraid," an acknowledgment of the doubts and at the same time an encouragement to step out and try anyway. Have you ever thought of where our Christian faith might have gone had the disciples been afraid to tell the story? Or what about countless generations of witnesses who have told and lived out the story, often in fear, until it reached our ears for the first time? Christ is risen! God is with us, in this time and this place and calling us to rise above the doubts and even the fears and then to dare to be followers of Jesus Christ. It is our turn, you know—to acknowledge the doubt, the fear, and to step out in faith. "Then Jesus said to them, 'Do not be afraid; go and tell my brothers and sisters to go to Galilee [to step out on the journey]; there they will see me.'"

Are you afraid? Me, too. Let's step out anyway; it will be worth the risk.

Jerry D. Smith

Pray for the vitality of your faith community and other communities of faith so that we all might behave in alignment with the reality that we are raised with Christ.

Begin with the prayer for guidance and discernment you wrote on Day 1.

Read Mark 16:1–8 slowly and prayerfully. What words or phrases stand out for you?

When the Sabbath was over, Mary Magdalene, and Mary the mother of James, and Salome bought spices, so that they might go and anoint him. ²And very early on the first day of the week, when the sun had risen, they went to the tomb. ³They had been saying to one another, "Who will roll away the stone for us from the entrance to the tomb?" ⁴When they looked up, they saw that the stone, which was very large, had already been rolled back. ⁵As they entered the tomb, they saw a young man, dressed in a white robe, sitting on the right side; and they were alarmed. ⁶But he said to them, "Do not be alarmed; you are looking for Jesus of Nazareth, who was crucified. He has been raised; he is not here. Look, there is the place they laid him. ⁷But go, tell his disciples and Peter that he is going ahead of you to Galilee; there you will see him, just as he told you." ⁸So they went out and fled from the tomb, for terror and amazement had seized them; and they said nothing to anyone, for they were afraid.

⁹Now after he rose early on the first day of the week, he appeared first to Mary Magdalene, from whom he had cast out seven demons. ¹⁰She went out and told those who had been with him, while they were mourning and weeping. ¹¹But when they heard that he was alive and had been seen by her, they would not believe it.

¹²After this he appeared in another form to two of them, as they were walking into the country. ¹³And they went back and told the rest, but they did not believe them.

¹⁴Later he appeared to the eleven themselves as they were sitting at the table; and he upbraided them for their lack of faith and stubbornness, because they had not believed those who saw him after he had risen. ¹⁵And he said to them, "Go into all the world and proclaim the good news to the whole creation. ¹⁶The one who believes and is baptized will be saved; but the one who does not believe will be condemned. ¹⁷And these signs will accompany those who believe: by using my name they will cast out demons; they will speak in new tongues; ¹⁸they will pick up snakes in their hands, and if they drink any deadly thing, it will not hurt them; they will lay their hands on the sick, and they will recover."

Reflect

How did you respond the first time you heard the proclamation that Jesus had risen?

In our postmodern world, how is it possible for people to accept the good news of Christ's resurrection?

What role does fear play in your struggle to be an agent of God's mission in the world?

Respond

Prepare a one-minute testimony from your experience that might cause a person to consider the possibility of the resurrection so that more might understand that we are raised with Christ

Encouragement: *What If?*

There had been an automobile accident. A child had been crippled. And a United Methodist man named Jim heard God telling him, he said, to go to the hospital and lay hands on the child, and heal him.

But he was on his way to work — he could do it on the way home, couldn't he? Wouldn't that be better? Yes, definitely, that would make much more sense.

That evening, though, the voice of God seemed more distant, the prompting less sure. He didn't go to the hospital at all. And was haunted by that decision.

What if …?

Since hearing Jim tell his story, years ago, I have been haunted by it, too. And by the realization that I would have done exactly the same.

Was it a fanciful notion on Jim's part that God would instruct him to perform a healing? Is such a thing even possible? And does God deliver messages like that today?

Mark 16:17-18 says, "And these signs will accompany those who believe: by using my name they will cast out demons; they will speak in new tongues; they will pick up snakes in their hands, and if they drink any deadly thing, it will not hurt them; they will lay their hands on the sick, and they will recover."

Perhaps Jesus was speaking to first century believers alone. Perhaps he was speaking metaphorically. Or maybe I, like the disciples, should be upbraided for "lack of faith, and stubbornness."

I don't know … But it makes me wonder.

What if …?

Cate Monaghan

Pray that God would remove any fear that is keeping you from sharing that testimony when the opportunity presents itself.

Begin with the prayer for guidance and discernment you wrote on Day 1.

Read Luke 24:1–12 slowly and prayerfully. What words or phrases stand out for you?

> But on the first day of the week, at early dawn, they came to the tomb, taking the spices that they had prepared. ²They found the stone rolled away from the tomb, ³but when they went in, they did not find the body. ⁴While they were perplexed about this, suddenly two men in dazzling clothes stood beside them. ⁵The women were terrified and bowed their faces to the ground, but the men said to them, "Why do you look for the living among the dead? He is not here, but has risen. ⁶Remember how he told you, while he was still in Galilee, ⁷that the Son of Man must be handed over to sinners, and be crucified, and on the third day rise again." ⁸Then they remembered his words, ⁹and returning from the tomb, they told all this to the eleven and to all the rest. ¹⁰Now it was Mary Magdalene, Joanna, Mary the mother of James, and the other women with them who told this to the apostles. ¹¹But these words seemed to them an idle tale, and they did not believe them. ¹²But Peter got up and ran to the tomb; stooping and looking in, he saw the linen cloths by themselves; then he went home, amazed at what had happened.

Reflect

How is the reality of the resurrection validated in your life?

What adjustments, if any, do you need to make in your thinking or acting which would make the resurrection of Jesus more central in your life? In your church?

Could you be missing an important witness because you don't value the source (i.e., "it seems to you an idle tale")?

Respond

Share the one-minute testimony you wrote yesterday with someone who has recently experienced loss.

Encouragement: *Remember the Words of God*

The women became witnesses to the resurrection of Jesus when they remembered what Jesus had said. We need to remember the words of God to be the agents of God's Kingdom. What did God say? God did not guarantee a trouble-free life. God did say that we would face troubles! God did say that we would have challenges. However, God also said that if we would follow God's words God would be with us! To be the agencies of the movement that God is making, we have to remember what God has said! Let us go back to the words of God! Otherwise, even when you see the empty tomb, you will just go home, amazed with what has happened!

Sungho Lee

Pray that your heart and the hearts of all who are sharing in this study would be "strangely warmed" by the risen Christ.

Begin with the prayer for guidance and discernment you wrote on Day 1.

Read Acts 10:34–43 slowly and prayerfully. What words or phrases stand out for you?

> Then Peter began to speak to them [i.e. the Gentile Cornelius and his household]: "I truly understand that God shows no partiality, ³⁵but in every nation anyone who fears him and does what is right is acceptable to him. ³⁶You know the message he sent to the people of Israel, preaching peace by Jesus Christ—he is Lord of all. ³⁷That message spread throughout Judea, beginning in Galilee after the baptism that John announced: ³⁸how God anointed Jesus of Nazareth with the Holy Spirit and with power; how he went about doing good and healing all who were oppressed by the devil, for God was with him. ³⁹We are witnesses to all that he did both in Judea and in Jerusalem. They put him to death by hanging him on a tree; ⁴⁰but God raised him on the third day and allowed him to appear, ⁴¹not to all the people but to us who were chosen by God as witnesses, and who ate and drank with him after he rose from the dead. ⁴²He commanded us to preach to the people and to testify that he is the one ordained by God as judge of the living and the dead. ⁴³All the prophets testify about him that everyone who believes in him receives forgiveness of sins through his name."

Reflect

According to Peter's proclamation what are the implications of the resurrection?

How would you sum up the story of Jesus and his significance to the world in 50 words or less?

Even though Peter is a witness to Christ, he has a kind of conversion of thinking through his encounter with the Gentile Cornelius. What was the last encounter you had which caused you to rethink the implications of your faith?

Respond

Be open to the fact that people you encounter today are potential instruments of the Holy Spirit, leading you to new understandings about God and your resurrection faith.

Encouragement: *Father Abraham Had Many Sons*

> *"Father Abraham had many sons.*
> *Many sons had Father Abraham.*
> *I am one of them. And so are you.*
> *So let's just praise the Lord."*

That was the song that greeted our van as we drove up to the little Methodist church in Desire, Jamaica. There were four of us, in mission together to offer a vacation Bible school to any young people in the area who wanted to come. After navigating the windy road, we stepped out in the warm sunshine and heard the sound of children's voices....

"I am one of them. And so are you...."

I felt tears in my eyes. You see, I had thought that I was coming to share my faith, but instead, I discovered God was already there. The testimony of faith came from the children, who were sitting politely in the pews, waiting for us. These same children had pumped the water for their families from the local well that morning. By the world's standards, they didn't have much. But they had more than enough faith to share with us.

God's message is for everybody. That's what Peter said. The Message puts these words in his mouth: "Nothing could be plainer: God plays no favorites! It makes no difference who you are, or where you're from…." How I embrace that word! We United Methodists in this part of the world claim and live deeply in our diversity. Our proclamation comes in many languages and expressions that we know are pleasing to God. What a joy when we see Christ in one another.

And what sorrow when we fail to see, fully, what God sees in each of us, what God has forgiven in every one of God's beloved children — the young ones, the older ones, the ones who look like me and the ones who don't, the ones who pray without ceasing in their simple homes or shelters, the ones whose politics or perspectives are different from mine, those whose mistakes in life are written in bad decisions that fill the news.

It's the most basic of our faith claims: Christ died for each of these, lives in every one. Sung in grand hymns or a children's song, it's still the same Easter promise. It seems to me that only when I truly claim that Gospel hope for myself in its fullness, can I see the Christ in you and in them and in us. Lord, bless us into receiving Easter deeply into our very beings, that we might live it out into the world.

Kristie Olah

Pray that your church and all churches would truly have "open doors," show no partiality and exhibit radical hospitality. That we would behave in a way which clearly shows we are raised with Christ.

Begin with the prayer for guidance and discernment you wrote on Day 1.

Read 1 Corinthians 15:1–26 slowly and prayerfully. What words or phrases stand out for you?

Now I would remind you, brothers and sisters, of the good news that I proclaimed to you, which you in turn received, in which also you stand, ²through which also you are being saved, if you hold firmly to the message that I proclaimed to you—unless you have come to believe in vain. ³For I handed on to you as of first importance what I in turn had received: that Christ died for our sins in accordance with the scriptures, ⁴and that he was buried, and that he was raised on the third day in accordance with the scriptures, ⁵and that he appeared to Cephas, then to the twelve. ⁶Then he appeared to more than five hundred brothers and sisters at one time, most of whom are still alive, though some have died. ⁷Then he appeared to James, then to all the apostles. ⁸Last of all, as to one untimely born, he appeared also to me. ⁹For I am the least of the apostles, unfit to be called an apostle, because I persecuted the church of God. ¹⁰But by the grace of God I am what I am, and his grace toward me has not been in vain. On the contrary, I worked harder than any of them—though it was not I, but the grace of God that is with me. ¹¹Whether then it was I or they, so we proclaim and so you have come to believe.

¹²Now if Christ is proclaimed as raised from the dead, how can some of you say there is no resurrection of the dead? ¹³If there is no resurrection of the dead, then Christ has not been raised; ¹⁴and if Christ has not been raised, then our proclamation has been in vain and your faith has been in vain. ¹⁵We are even found to be misrepresenting God, because we testified of God that he raised Christ—whom he did not raise if it is true that the dead are not raised. ¹⁶For if the dead are not raised, then Christ has not been raised. ¹⁷If Christ has not been raised, your faith is futile and you are still in your sins. ¹⁸Then those also who have died in Christ have perished. ¹⁹If for this life only we have hoped in Christ, we are of all people most to be pitied.

²⁰But in fact Christ has been raised from the dead, the first fruits of those who have died. ²¹For since death came through a human being, the resurrection of the dead has also come through a human being; ²²for as all die in Adam, so all will be made alive in Christ. ²³But each in his own order: Christ the first fruits, then

at his coming those who belong to Christ. ²⁴Then comes the end, when he hands over the kingdom to God the Father, after he has destroyed every ruler and every authority and power. ²⁵For he must reign until he has put all his enemies under his feet. ²⁶The last enemy to be destroyed is death.

Reflect

Basically, Paul seems to be saying that our entire faith rises or falls on the resurrection of Christ. Do you agree?

How does Paul's point of view differ from someone who sees faith purely in moral terms?

What is the connection between Christ's resurrection and ours?

Respond

Make as many attitude adjustments as necessary in light of the promise that "in Christ you shall be made alive."

Encouragement: *Paul and the Resurrection*

Paul is very clear about the significance of the resurrection. I have no doubt Paul said what needed to be said to the people who needed to hear it.

I've never had much clarity around the significance of the resurrection. I love Advent, I get Christmas. The significance of Easter always seemed fear-based, significant only to the extent we are afraid of death. Nevertheless, I knew I was missing something truly important since so many people I admire find great meaning in the resurrection.

Last week, as I felt my way forward toward Easter once again, I caught a glimmer of it. I put myself into the stories of Holy Week as usual, and this time they became real. Christ's death and resurrection are gifts I was able to receive, not explain.

Gone is the abyss between myself and God, gone the need for apologetic bridges. There is no abyss. Christ is risen indeed.

Diane Knudsen

Pray for the renewing of your mind in light of Christ's resurrection so that you might be more aware that you are raised with Christ.

Begin with the prayer for guidance and discernment you wrote on Day 1.

Read Colossians 3:1–4 slowly and prayerfully. What words or phrases stand out for you?

> So if you have been raised with Christ, seek the things that are above, where Christ is, seated at the right hand of God. [2]Set your minds on things that are above, not on things that are on earth, [3]for you have died, and your life is hidden with Christ in God. [4]When Christ who is your life is revealed, then you also will be revealed with him in glory.

Reflect

On a typical day, what do you seek? How often do you "seek the things that are above?"

What does it mean that you have died and your life is hidden with Christ in God (v. 3)?

What is the evidence in your life that you have been raised with Christ?

Respond

Intentionally (re)set your mind on "things above," three times today (perhaps around meals). Then reflect on how well your mind has been set on "things above" between those times.

Encouragement: *Focus*

In the first century the earth gets a bad rap.

Is resurrection really about focusing "above" in opposition to the things of earth?

Christ redeems creation — meaning the earthly things, as well as things above. Matthew describes it as "the curtain of the temple is torn in two." We can see things as they are — not the least of which is the divinely infused earth and the divinely infused life we live.

It is no less of a struggle to see the Divine around us than, in Paul's language, to focus on "things above." The task is just more immediate than we might think.

Ted Virts

Pray for a deep desire to seek the things that are above. Pray that your Easter faith (i.e., believing that you are raised with Christ) reaches so deep that you feel it and desire it.

Week 2

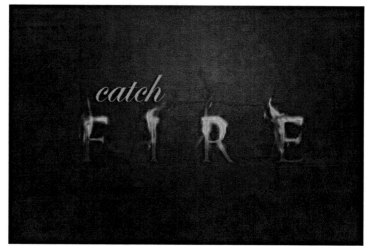

This week we start the pattern that we will carry through the rest of the 50 days.

That pattern is to surround our reading of the book of Acts (Monday through Friday) with a reading from the Gospel (on Sunday) and First Peter (on Saturday).

Our encounter with Jesus through the Gospel text is the spark that ignites a fire, which spreads (as in the book of Acts) and is sustained (with resources such as those mentioned in First Peter).

The readings this week proclaim that we are Spirit-filled people who have been sent by Jesus to be his witnesses (John and Acts). Catching fire is more than just an internal process. It changes everything from our outlook to our openness to others to our alignment with God's plans to our relationships.

"We have been born anew to a living hope through the resurrection of Jesus Christ from the dead …." (First Peter 1:3)

From about half past ten at night until about half past twelve … FIRE … GOD of Abraham, GOD of Isaac, GOD of Jacob… not of the philosophers and of the learned. Certitude. Certitude. Feeling. Joy. Peace.

GOD of Jesus Christ. My God and your God. Your GOD will be my God. Forgetfulness of the world and of everything, except GOD… Joy, joy, joy, tears of joy.

Jesus Christ. Jesus Christ. … Renunciation, total and sweet. Complete submission to Jesus Christ and to my director. Eternally in joy for a day's exercise on the earth.

I will not forget thy word. Amen.

Blaise Pascal (from his journal),
17th century French mathematician,
physicist and philosopher

It is not light that we need, but fire; it is not the gentle shower, but thunder. We need the storm, the whirlwind, and the earthquake.

Frederick Douglas,
19th century American social reformer

Pray for guidance and discernment. If you wish, write that prayer here and use it for the next six days.

Read John 20:19–31 slowly and prayerfully. What words or phrases stand out for you?

> When it was evening on that day, the first day of the week, and the doors of the house where the disciples had met were locked for fear of the Jews, Jesus came and stood among them and said, "Peace be with you." 20After he said this, he showed them his hands and his side. Then the disciples rejoiced when they saw the Lord. 21Jesus said to them again, "Peace be with you. As the Father has sent me, so I send you." 22When he had said this, he breathed on them and said to them, "Receive the Holy Spirit. 23If you forgive the sins of any, they are forgiven them; if you retain the sins of any, they are retained." 24But Thomas (who was called the Twin), one of the twelve, was not with them when Jesus came. 25So the other disciples told him, "We have seen the Lord." But he said to them, "Unless I see the mark of the nails in his hands, and put my finger in the mark of the nails and my hand in his side, I will not believe."
>
> 26A week later his disciples were again in the house, and Thomas was with them. Although the doors were shut, Jesus came and stood among them and said, "Peace be with you." 27Then he said to Thomas, "Put your finger here and see my hands. Reach out your hand and put it in my side. Do not doubt but believe." 28Thomas answered him, "My Lord and my God!" 29Jesus said to him, "Have you believed because you have seen me? Blessed are those who have not seen and yet have come to believe." 30Now Jesus did many other signs in the presence of his disciples, which are not written in this book. 31But these are written so that you may come to believe that Jesus is the Messiah, the Son of God, and that through believing you may have life in his name.

Reflect

In what part of your life do you need the peace of Christ right now?

Where is Jesus sending you today? To do what? What is the role of the Holy Spirit in this mission?

Are you struggling with any doubts? If so, what are they?

Respond

Live today fully aware that you have received the Holy Spirit and are sent by Jesus. Notice what is different in how you approach your work, relationships, family and community.

Encouragement: *Close Encounters*

Caravaggio's painting of "Doubting Thomas" is world famous. In it Jesus lets Thomas get up close to see his wounds. Thomas is bent over, eye-level with the wound in Jesus' side, and Jesus is guiding his hand so that he might feel the wound for himself. You can just see Jesus telling him, "Reach out your hand and put it in my side. Do not doubt, but believe."

We can all identify with that painting because every one of us wants to have an experience with Jesus that is concrete and tangible. Jesus said to Thomas, "Have you believed because you have seen me? Blessed are those who have not seen and yet have come to believe."

As the community of faith, we are the continuing evidence of the resurrection. It is remarkable that here, 2000 years after the fact, the stories about what Jesus did and said are still told; that in spite of the distance of space and time of the modern world, people are still led to proclaim with Thomas, "my Lord and my God."

Thomas Merton said, "A true encounter with Christ liberates something in us, a power we did not know we had, a hope, a capacity for life, a resilience, an ability to bounce back when we thought we were completely defeated, a capacity to grow and change, a power of creative transformation."

It is a creative transformation of a world that begins in each single transformed heart, an encounter with the Risen Lord that we might have hope, and who then commissioned us as the church and empowered us to share the good news of the resurrection to a lost and fragmented world.

Jerry Smith

Pray for the mission of your church—to make disciples of Jesus Christ who transform the world—and for your people to catch that fire.

Begin with the prayer for guidance and discernment you wrote on Day 8.

Read Acts 1:1–11 slowly and prayerfully. What words or phrases stand out for you?

> In the first book, Theophilus, I wrote about all that Jesus did and taught from the beginning ²until the day when he was taken up to heaven, after giving instructions through the Holy Spirit to the apostles whom he had chosen. ³After his suffering he presented himself alive to them by many convincing proofs, appearing to them during forty days and speaking about the kingdom of God. ⁴While staying with them, he ordered them not to leave Jerusalem, but to wait there for the promise of the Father. "This," he said, "is what you have heard from me; ⁵for John baptized with water, but you will be baptized with the Holy Spirit not many days from now."
>
> ⁶So when they had come together, they asked him, "Lord, is this the time when you will restore the kingdom to Israel?" ⁷He replied, "It is not for you to know the times or periods that the Father has set by his own authority. ⁸But you will receive power when the Holy Spirit has come upon you; and you will be my witnesses in Jerusalem, in all Judea and Samaria, and to the ends of the earth." ⁹When he had said this, as they were watching, he was lifted up, and a cloud took him out of their sight. ¹⁰While he was going and they were gazing up toward heaven, suddenly two men in white robes stood by them. ¹¹They said, "Men of Galilee, why do you stand looking up toward heaven? This Jesus, who has been taken up from you into heaven, will come in the same way as you saw him go into heaven."

Reflect

What kind of power do you receive when the Holy Spirit comes upon you? What is the nature of this power? What does it accomplish? What is its purpose?

Where is your Jerusalem? Judea? Samaria? Ends of the earth?

Where do you feel called to be Christ's witness today? What form might it take? Are you prepared to be His witness if the opportunity is available?

Respond

Share your reflections from today's devotional with a friend or on face-book.com/catchfire50

Encouragement: *THEY — Is Us*

Acts 1:9 says, "…as THEY were watching, he was lifted up, and a cloud took him out of their sight."

Had I been one of the "THEY" who were watching Jesus be elevated up and away, I would have just "thrown in the towel." I would have said, "Okay, Lord God, Cloud, Spirit, Jesus Christ, Savior, Mystery — we have already been through a lot together — and now, this."

Had I been one of the "THEY," I would have said, "I "throw in the towel" to you. Your power, your big picture perspective, your Salvation Kingdom is so much more than I can comprehend. I get it. I'm in."

It is the same, when I see someone being lifted up in that same power in which Jesus was lifted.

I just experienced a "Sunday after Easter" sermon preached by a lay person from Oakhurst. She testified to her having lived a worldly/culturally fine but spiritually empty life — until she was drawn back to a worshipping community. On that first Sunday, she remembered sitting on that back pew of the church, and putting on her sunglasses as she was reawakening to and weeping in the Holy Spirit power. In the time to come, she became a part of that church community where she learned, grew, shared, was nurtured, and was lifted to a more full life and calling.

Recently, this laywoman felt the call to hone her gifts for ministry and has completed Conference Lay Ministry training. This is training that she is now using in her local church. She is unsure of where this may lead in the fullness of her spiritual life, except that the Spirit continues to lift her up. She continues to be lifted by the Holy Spirit.

What a blessing, once again, to be a part of the "THEY!" And again, I respond, "I get it. I'm in! Thanks be to God!!"

Mariellen Yoshino

Pray for the power of the Holy Spirit to catch fire in you today so that you might ignite others with your witness.

Begin with the prayer for guidance and discernment you wrote on Day 8.

Read Acts 1:12–26 slowly and prayerfully. What words or phrases stand out for you?

> Then they returned to Jerusalem from the mount called Olivet, which is near Jerusalem, a Sabbath day's journey away. ¹³When they had entered the city, they went to the room upstairs where they were staying, Peter, and John, and James, and Andrew, Philip and Thomas, Bartholomew and Matthew, James son of Alphaeus, and Simon the Zealot, and Judas son of James. ¹⁴All these were constantly devoting themselves to prayer, together with certain women, including Mary the mother of Jesus, as well as his brothers.
>
> ¹⁵In those days Peter stood up among the believers (together the crowd numbered about one hundred twenty persons) and said, ¹⁶"Friends, the scripture had to be fulfilled, which the Holy Spirit through David foretold concerning Judas, who became a guide for those who arrested Jesus— ¹⁷for he was numbered among us and was allotted his share in this ministry." ¹⁸(Now this man acquired a field with the reward of his wickedness; and falling headlong, he burst open in the middle and all his bowels gushed out. ¹⁹This became known to all the residents of Jerusalem, so that the field was called in their language Hakeldama, that is, Field of Blood.) ²⁰"For it is written in the book of Psalms, 'Let his homestead become desolate, and let there be no one to live in it'; and 'Let another take his position of overseer.' ²¹So one of the men who have accompanied us during all the time that the Lord Jesus went in and out among us, ²²beginning from the baptism of John until the day when he was taken up from us—one of these must become a witness with us to his resurrection." ²³So they proposed two, Joseph called Barsabbas, who was also known as Justus, and Matthias. ²⁴Then they prayed and said, "Lord, you know everyone's heart. Show us which one of these two you have chosen ²⁵to take the place in this ministry and apostleship from which Judas turned aside to go to his own place." ²⁶And they cast lots for them, and the lot fell on Matthias; and he was added to the eleven apostles.

Reflect

Who are your partners in ministry?

Who else do you need as a partner?

How does the text provide instructions we can use when finding new partners for mission?

Respond

Affirm one of your partners in ministry today. Make a list of potential partners and begin a process of discernment, so that you know whom you might approach to become a partner in the near future.

Encouragement: *Prayer Partners*

As I read today's devotional and thought about the question, "Who are your partners in ministry?" several people came to mind: My colleagues in my office, my camp staff, the youth workers at the local churches, and the many local pastors with whom I have the privilege of working. I thought and prayed about the thought of which other people could come forth as a partner in our ministry and to strengthen God's mission and movement in our world. Then I came across an article about the power of prayer partners:

Some months ago I enjoyed a four-week summer sabbatical. I set three goals during the month. First, I wanted to plan an autumn series of lessons on grace (which I did). Second, I aspired to break ninety on the golf course (I did that too — once). And third, I wanted to learn more about leadership skills. It was through this third goal that I came to know John Maxwell.

A coworker recommended I seek his advice, so I gave him a call. He invited me to come and speak to the Skyline congregation in San Diego. I did. I gathered some ideas on leadership, but much more, I gained a passion for Prayer Partners.

My Sunday at Skyline was bathed in prayer. The Prayer Partners met me as I walked in the door and met me as I walked off the platform. They were praying for me as I flew, as I spoke, even as I rested. I was so convicted about the importance of Prayer Partners that I asked God to grant me 120 members who would covenant to pray for me daily and pray with me fervently.

Upon returning to the pulpit I announced my dream to the congregation. Within a month exactly 120 people had volunteered to form the team. We divided the volunteers into four groups and assigned each group one Sunday per month on which they would arrive early and pray for the congregation.

That was six months ago. Has God honored the prayers of his people? Here is a sample of what God has done since we organized Prayer Partners:

- We have broken our Sunday attendance record twice.
- We finished the year with our highest ever average Sunday attendance.
- We finished the year — hang on to your hat — over budget.

- We added three new staff members and six new elders.
- We witnessed several significant healings.
- I completed a challenging book on grace.
- Our church antagonism is down, and church unity is high.

And most significantly, we called the church to forty days of prayer and fasting, inviting God to shine his face upon us. God has honored the prayers of his people. More than ever I'm convinced: **When we work, we work; but when we pray, God works.** [Emphasis mine.]

From Max Ludado's Forward to Prayer Partners by John Maxwell

A simple way to invite others to "catch" or "re-light" the fire…"will you be my ministry partner though prayer?"

Kelly Newell

Pray that God would send you new partners in ministry and give thanks for those you already have; that you all would catch fire (or get re-lit) in a way which allows you to join the movement of God's mission in the world.

Begin with the prayer for guidance and discernment you wrote on Day 8.

Read Acts 2:1–13 slowly and prayerfully. What words or phrases stand out for you?

> *When the day of Pentecost had come, they were all together in one place. ²And suddenly from heaven there came a sound like the rush of a violent wind, and it filled the entire house where they were sitting. ³Divided tongues, as of fire, appeared among them, and a tongue rested on each of them. ⁴All of them were filled with the Holy Spirit and began to speak in other languages, as the Spirit gave them ability.*
>
> *⁵Now there were devout Jews from every nation under heaven living in Jerusalem. ⁶And at this sound the crowd gathered and was bewildered, because each one heard them speaking in the native language of each. ⁷Amazed and astonished, they asked, "Are not all these who are speaking Galileans? ⁸And how is it that we hear, each of us, in our own native language? ⁹Parthians, Medes, Elamites, and residents of Mesopotamia, Judea and Cappadocia, Pontus and Asia, ¹⁰Phrygia and Pamphylia, Egypt and the parts of Libya belonging to Cyrene, and visitors from Rome, both Jews and proselytes, ¹¹Cretans and Arabs—in our own languages we hear them speaking about God's deeds of power." ¹²All were amazed and perplexed, saying to one another, "What does this mean?" ¹³But others sneered and said, "They are filled with new wine."*

Reflect

What impact does the image of the Holy Spirit coming as "tongues of fire" have on you? What is the nature of fire and how does that relate to the Holy Spirit?

How would you answer the question in verse 12, "What does this mean?"

What is the relevance of Pentecost for churches which want to become a movement of God's mission in the world again?

Respond

Learn something today about or from a person who is of a different culture than you.

Encouragement: *Speaking in Other Languages*

As a communicator, I love this passage. The Spirit came upon them as tongues of fire and gave voice to each one, to speak "in other languages, as the Spirit gave them ability."

God made all of us communicators that day, and it was no casual gift! The dramatic way in which it was bestowed speaks to the importance of what happened. God wants us to take communicating seriously.

Today the new languages in which we are asked to be conversant can seem forbidding: Facebook, texting, Twitter … tomorrow's latest and greatest thing. But we aren't hanging out there by ourselves. The Spirit "gave them ability" and gives ability to us. We have been touched by tongues of fire! What a powerful image that is.

But to me the best part of the passage is the second part of verse 11, when the crowd, amazed and astonished, says, "… we hear them declaring the wonders of God in our own tongues!" (NIV)

Can't you just hear — not just the wonder, but also the delight in their voices? "They're speaking my language! They care enough about me to connect with me in ways that I can understand!"

Who wouldn't want to be a part of that?

Cate Monaghan

Pray that churches and other faith communities have a fresh experience of being filled with the Holy Spirit and catch fire.

Begin with the prayer for guidance and discernment you wrote on Day 8.

Read Acts 2:14–36 slowly and prayerfully. What words or phrases stand out for you?

> But Peter, standing with the eleven, raised his voice and addressed them, "Men of Judea and all who live in Jerusalem, let this be known to you, and listen to what I say. ¹⁵Indeed, these are not drunk, as you suppose, for it is only nine o"clock in the morning. ¹⁶No, this is what was spoken through the prophet Joel: ¹⁷'In the last days it will be, God declares, that I will pour out my Spirit upon all flesh, and your sons and your daughters shall prophesy, and your young men shall see visions, and your old men shall dream dreams. ¹⁸Even upon my slaves, both men and women, in those days I will pour out my Spirit; and they shall prophesy. ¹⁹And I will show portents in the heaven above and signs on the earth below, blood, and fire, and smoky mist. ²⁰The sun shall be turned to darkness and the moon to blood, before the coming of the Lord's great and glorious day. ²¹Then everyone who calls on the name of the Lord shall be saved.' ²²"You that are Israelites, listen to what I have to say: Jesus of Nazareth, a man attested to you by God with deeds of power, wonders, and signs that God did through him among you, as you yourselves know— ²³this man, handed over to you according to the definite plan and foreknowledge of God, you crucified and killed by the hands of those outside the law. ²⁴But God raised him up, having freed him from death, because it was impossible for him to be held in its power. ²⁵For David says concerning him, 'I saw the Lord always before me, for he is at my right hand so that I will not be shaken; ²⁶therefore my heart was glad, and my tongue rejoiced; moreover my flesh will live in hope. ²⁷For you will not abandon my soul to Hades, or let your Holy One experience corruption. ²⁸You have made known to me the ways of life; you will make me full of gladness with your presence.' ²⁹"Fellow Israelites, I may say to you confidently of our ancestor David that he both died and was buried, and his tomb is with us to this day. ³⁰Since he was a prophet, he knew that God had sworn with an oath to him that he would put one of his descendants on his throne. ³¹Foreseeing this, David spoke of the resurrection of the Messiah, saying, 'He was not abandoned to Hades, nor did his flesh experience corruption.' ³²This Jesus God raised up, and of that all of us are witnesses. ³³Being therefore exalted at the right hand of God, and having received from the Father the promise of the Holy Spirit, he has poured out this that you both see and hear. ³⁴For David did not ascend into the heavens, but he himself says, 'The Lord said to my Lord, "Sit

at my right hand, ³⁵until I make your enemies your footstool.'" ³⁶Therefore let the entire house of Israel know with certainty that God has made him both Lord and Messiah, this Jesus whom you crucified."

Reflect

What are the main points of Peter's message?

How have you experienced the reality of God's promises being fulfilled in your life?

What does it mean to you that Jesus is both Lord and Christ (vs. 36)?

Respond

Let Jesus be Lord in an area of your life which you haven't completely surrendered to His reign.

Encouragement: *The Wait Is Over*

As I reflect on Peter's message to his community in Acts 2:14-36 one phrase and an old, old story come to mind.

"The wait is over" is the phrase that comes to mind when I reflect on Peter's message. Peter embraces all that the community has known in tradition and leadership and affirms that God has made Jesus both Lord and Messiah.

Now for the old story:

Once there was a man whose house was in a flood. He stood on the porch as the waters rose. A boat came by. The driver urged the man to get on board but the man said he was waiting on the Lord to save him. The waters rose, the first floor was flooded and as the man looked out his second story window, another boat came to rescue him. The man turned the boat away, saying he would wait for God to rescue him. Finally he was clinging to the chimney on the roof. A helicopter flew overhead and dropped down a ladder. The man waved it off, saying Jesus would save his life. Finally he was swept away in the waters and drowned. At the pearly gates, he saw God and said, "Lord, all my life I did as you asked but when the time came you did not save me." And God said, "I sent you two boats and a helicopter; what else did you want?"

God has been and will always be active in the world. Sometimes we can't put all the pieces together to see it. Peter put the pieces together for his community and said to them — you have all you have been promised and more. The wait is over!

I give thanks on this day for all who labor to point others to our Lord and Savior. And I pray that as a community of faith we can truly be more about fanning the flames than waiting for a spark that has, in fact, already been ignited.

Linda Caldwell

Pray that Jesus is Lord and Christ in every area of your life and your faith community. Ask God to show you areas in which Jesus may not be Lord, and pray for a transformation in this area so that more of you might catch fire.

Begin with the prayer for guidance and discernment you wrote on Day 8.

Read Acts 2:37–47 slowly and prayerfully. What words or phrases stand out for you?

> Now when they heard this, they were cut to the heart and said to Peter and to the other apostles, "Brothers, what should we do?" 38Peter said to them, "Repent, and be baptized every one of you in the name of Jesus Christ so that your sins may be forgiven; and you will receive the gift of the Holy Spirit. 39For the promise is for you, for your children, and for all who are far away, everyone whom the Lord our God calls to him." ⁴⁰And he testified with many other arguments and exhorted them, saying, "Save yourselves from this corrupt generation." ⁴¹So those who welcomed his message were baptized, and that day about three thousand persons were added.
>
> ⁴²They devoted themselves to the apostles' teaching and fellowship, to the breaking of bread and the prayers. ⁴³Awe came upon everyone, because many wonders and signs were being done by the apostles. ⁴⁴All who believed were together and had all things in common; ⁴⁵they would sell their possessions and goods and distribute the proceeds to all, as any had need. ⁴⁶Day by day, as they spent much time together in the temple, they broke bread at home and ate their food with glad and generous hearts, ⁴⁷praising God and having the goodwill of all the people. And day by day the Lord added to their number those who were being saved.

Reflect

Have you ever been "cut to the heart" when hearing the Good News about Jesus? What did you do?

Is there any obstacle in your life preventing you from receiving the full gift of the Holy Spirit? If so, what do you need to do to remove it?

How is your church like or unlike the fellowship of believers described in verses 42-47? What can you do to make it more like this?

Respond

Do one thing that makes your church or small group feel more like the fellowship of believers described in verses 42-47. If you are not in a small group during these 50 days, consider joining or starting one. (See the Small Group Template at the end of this devotional, which can be a guide for your small group meetings.)

Encouragement: *Witness and Action*

In this passage, Luke demonstrates the power of the Holy Spirit that gives us the capacity for the hallmark of the people called Methodist: Witness and Action. I notice that the first paragraph speaks of the witness, not only of Peter, but also the other apostles. Their message? "The promise is for you, your children and all who are 'far away' (from relationship to God). In the second paragraph, Luke offers his witness of what the promise lived out can look like: shared presence, faith, possessions, goods, worship, funds, generosity, hospitality...

"Cut to the heart?" Yes — When I imagine what Jesus Christ could accomplish through his Church if every United Methodist was so filled with God's Spirit. Surely, as in the early Church, sharing the promise of the Holy Spirit's power with someone who hasn't "known" God's presence and power would lead to the kind of transformed lives that Luke bears witness to.

But Christ is risen and WE are baptized! We have received the power for the testimony and the witness. What will it take for us to harness the great gift of the power of God? What do we need to do that will invite United Methodists to reclaim our heritage of testifying to God's power and sharing all for the sake of the mission?

Renae Extrum-Fernandez

Pray for an outpouring of the Holy Spirit so that your community of faith can catch fire and be as vital as the first one mentioned here in the book of Acts.

Begin with the prayer for guidance and discernment you wrote on Day 8.

Read 1 Peter 1:1–12 slowly and prayerfully. What words or phrases stand out for you?

¹Peter, an apostle of Jesus Christ, To the exiles of the Dispersion in Pontus, Galatia, Cappadocia, Asia, and Bithynia, ²who have been chosen and destined by God the Father and sanctified by the Spirit to be obedient to Jesus Christ and to be sprinkled with his blood:

May grace and peace be yours in abundance.

³Blessed be the God and Father of our Lord Jesus Christ! By his great mercy he has given us a new birth into a living hope through the resurrection of Jesus Christ from the dead, ⁴and into an inheritance that is imperishable, undefiled, and unfading, kept in heaven for you, ⁵who are being protected by the power of God through faith for a salvation ready to be revealed in the last time. ⁶In this you rejoice, even if now for a little while you have had to suffer various trials, ⁷so that the genuineness of your faith—being more precious than gold that, though perishable, is tested by fire—may be found to result in praise and glory and honor when Jesus Christ is revealed. ⁸Although you have not seen him, you love him; and even though you do not see him now, you believe in him and rejoice with an indescribable and glorious joy, ⁹for you are receiving the outcome of your faith, the salvation of your souls.

¹⁰Concerning this salvation, the prophets who prophesied of the grace that was to be yours made careful search and inquiry, ¹¹inquiring about the person or time that the Spirit of Christ within them indicated, when it testified in advance to the sufferings destined for Christ and the subsequent glory. ¹²It was revealed to them that they were serving not themselves but you, in regard to the things that have now been announced to you through those who brought you good news by the Holy Spirit sent from heaven—things into which angels long to look!

Reflect

What kind of trials are you or your community of faith facing? Would you describe these pressures as coming from without or from within?

Given those trials, what part of this passage is an encouragement to you?

What is the source of your hope? How do you sustain it?

Respond

Spend 15 minutes three times today (maybe around meal times) to pause and give praise to God in the midst of your suffering (personal, congregational and/or wider-community). Express love to God for giving us "a new birth into a living hope through the resurrection of Jesus Christ from the dead."

Encouragement: *Receiving*

Chosen.
Destined.
Sanctified.
By his great mercy.
New birth.
Imperishable.
Undefiled.
Being protected.

Such a contrast to attaining, achieving, planning, succeeding, evaluating.

Faith and fire are about being acted upon.

Sometimes in our striving to do, build and make, we become too busy to receive what God would give. If we would pause long enough to notice what God would do, God might have an easier time doing it.

Ted Virts

Pray a prayer of praise and adoration to God who loves you and gives you hope through Jesus Christ.

Keep It Burning

Week 3

We who inherit the legacy of Christ are people of the warm heart. As the disciples' hearts burned on the road to Emmaus and ignited their ministries, so it is that a heart warmed by the presence of the resurrected Christ (Luke) results in an individual spiritual experience and emanates out in acts of healing, witness, boldness, justice, radical sharing (Acts) and holy living (First Peter).

Lean on God this week and trust Christ's presence in your life… and in the life of your church. Doing so will help keep your fire burning, and it will propel you to bring that fire to the people around you in authentic and relevant ways.

Christ has no body now, but yours.
No hands, no feet on earth, but yours.
Yours are the eyes through which
Christ looks compassion into the world.
Yours are the feet with which
Christ walks to do good.
Yours are the hands with which
Christ blesses the world.

Teresa of Avila,
16th century Spanish mystic

Pray for guidance and discernment. If you wish, write that prayer here and use it for the next six days.

Read Luke 24:13–35 slowly and prayerfully. What words or phrases stand out for you?

> ¹³Now on that same day two of them were going to a village called Emmaus, about seven miles* from Jerusalem, ¹⁴and talking with each other about all these things that had happened. ¹⁵While they were talking and discussing, Jesus himself came near and went with them, ¹⁶but their eyes were kept from recognizing him. ¹⁷And he said to them, 'What are you discussing with each other while you walk along?' They stood still, looking sad. ¹⁸Then one of them, whose name was Cleopas, answered him, 'Are you the only stranger in Jerusalem who does not know the things that have taken place there in these days?' ¹⁹He asked them, 'What things?' They replied, 'The things about Jesus of Nazareth, who was a prophet mighty in deed and word before God and all the people, ²⁰and how our chief priests and leaders handed him over to be condemned to death and crucified him. ²¹But we had hoped that he was the one to redeem Israel. Yes, and besides all this, it is now the third day since these things took place. ²²Moreover, some women of our group astounded us. They were at the tomb early this morning, ²³and when they did not find his body there, they came back and told us that they had indeed seen a vision of angels who said that he was alive. ²⁴Some of those who were with us went to the tomb and found it just as the women had said; but they did not see him.' ²⁵Then he said to them, 'Oh, how foolish you are, and how slow of heart to believe all that the prophets have declared! ²⁶Was it not necessary that the Messiah should suffer these things and then enter into his glory?' ²⁷Then beginning with Moses and all the prophets, he interpreted to them the things about himself in all the scriptures.
>
> ²⁸As they came near the village to which they were going, he walked ahead as if he were going on. ²⁹But they urged him strongly, saying, 'Stay with us, because it is almost evening and the day is now nearly over.' So he went in to stay with them. ³⁰When he was at the table with them, he took bread, blessed and broke it, and gave it to them. ³¹Then their eyes were opened, and they recognized him; and he vanished from their sight. ³²They said to each other, 'Were not our hearts burning within us while he was talking to us on the road, while he was opening the scriptures to us?'

33That same hour they got up and returned to Jerusalem; and they found the eleven and their companions gathered together. 34They were saying, 'The Lord has risen indeed, and he has appeared to Simon!' 35Then they told what had happened on the road, and how he had been made known to them in the breaking of the bread.

Reflect

Has there been a time recently in which you didn't recognize Christ's presence—but looking back now, you realize that He was there?

Wesley talked about his heart being "strangely warmed." The Emmaus disciples said their hearts were burning within them. How would you describe your encounter with Christ?

What is the significance of their eyes being opened at the breaking of the bread?

Respond

Be prepared to write down a specific moment today in which you recognize Christ's presence.

Encouragement: *Recognizing Jesus*

The story of the walk to Emmaus is haunting. It is also timeless.

As I contemplated the last time I was in the presence of Christ and didn't see him, it struck me: He had been sitting right in front of me for the last 20 minutes and had just left at the last train stop.

I had noticed him clearly before then. I noted his unshaved face. I saw his scuffed and worn shoes. I noted how his clothes had that ground-in dirt from sitting on things without upholstery. I noted the hand-stitched repairs on his pack.

I saw him but didn't recognize him.

I then looked over the coach I was sharing with 50 other people and pondered which one of them might be Christ also. Was he there?

There was the girl next to me, thumbing out a text discussion over her cell phone with some unseen person, oblivious to the people around her. The next person over was bobbing his head to the beat of some tune from the device wired into his ears. He was staring blankly at the back of the head in front of him.

As I scanned the faces before me I was not able to make eye contact with a single person, not one. And up to that moment I had been just like them.

For the next 30 minutes I watched as we all meticulously avoided looking at each other; avoided eye contact, avoided speaking, avoided acknowledging that any of us existed beyond an object to not bump into. I wanted to jump up and start telling them each that the Jesus in me loves the Jesus in you.

I didn't do that, but I felt it.

Then I caught a glance from a woman walking past. We looked briefly at each other. I smiled and nodded slightly at her — and I'm convinced that I got back more than a polite smile; it was more of a knowing wink, and a nod. It seemed to say, "I see you. I am Jesus, here in this woman, and I love you."

And then she was gone.

Phil Bandy

Pray that Christ would be fully revealed in the ordinary experiences of your day, to keep the fire of the Risen Christ burning.

Begin with the prayer for guidance and discernment you wrote on Day 15.

Read Acts 3:1–10 slowly and prayerfully. What words or phrases stand out for you?

> One day Peter and John were going up to the temple at the hour of prayer, at three o'clock in the afternoon. ²And a man lame from birth was being carried in. People would lay him daily at the gate of the temple called the Beautiful Gate so that he could ask for alms from those entering the temple. ³When he saw Peter and John about to go into the temple, he asked them for alms. ⁴Peter looked intently at him, as did John, and said, 'Look at us.' ⁵And he fixed his attention on them, expecting to receive something from them. ⁶But Peter said, 'I have no silver or gold, but what I have I give you; in the name of Jesus Christ of Nazareth, stand up and walk.' ⁷And he took him by the right hand and raised him up; and immediately his feet and ankles were made strong. ⁸Jumping up, he stood and began to walk, and he entered the temple with them, walking and leaping and praising God. ⁹All the people saw him walking and praising God, ¹⁰and they recognized him as the one who used to sit and ask for alms at the Beautiful Gate of the temple; and they were filled with wonder and amazement at what had happened to him.

Reflect

What is easy for you to freely give in your life? What is difficult?

What would it take for God to perform miracles of healing through you as he did through Peter and John?

What are you begging for?

Respond

Extend your hand to lift someone up today, in the name of Jesus.

Encouragement: *Accomplishing God's Mission*

Today we often find ourselves debating over how the mission of God is accomplished in the world. One side contends that the gospel should be taught first, and aid should come second. But there is also a growing contingent that suggests Jesus was much more concerned about the social injustices of his day, and that he used the channels of correcting those injustices as a means of reaching people with the gospel. That Jesus did this simply cannot be denied. But who says the two approaches are mutually exclusive?

What I find most unfortunate is that with all of this come the extremes. There are those who promote social justice at the expense of the gospel. And, to be sure, the other extreme exists — caring only about the gospel and little about social injustices.

Meeting certain needs before sharing the gospel isn't compromise, as some might suggest. It is one of a myriad of approaches that are both good and acceptable to God. The situation in our reflection warranted the approach, and that is good enough for me.

Jerry Smith

Pray, in the name of Jesus, for someone you know who needs healing—that the fire will start or keep burning in that person's life.

Begin with the prayer for guidance and discernment you wrote on Day 15.

Read Acts 3:11–26 slowly and prayerfully. What words or phrases stand out for you?

> *¹¹While he clung to Peter and John, all the people ran together to them in the portico called Solomon's Portico, utterly astonished. ¹²When Peter saw it, he addressed the people, 'You Israelites, why do you wonder at this, or why do you stare at us, as though by our own power or piety we had made him walk? ¹³The God of Abraham, the God of Isaac, and the God of Jacob, the God of our ancestors has glorified his servant Jesus, whom you handed over and rejected in the presence of Pilate, though he had decided to release him. ¹⁴But you rejected the Holy and Righteous One and asked to have a murderer given to you, ¹⁵and you killed the Author of life, whom God raised from the dead. To this we are witnesses. ¹⁶And by faith in his name, his name itself has made this man strong, whom you see and know; and the faith that is through Jesus has given him this perfect health in the presence of all of you.*

> *¹⁷And now, friends, I know that you acted in ignorance, as did also your rulers. ¹⁸In this way God fulfilled what he had foretold through all the prophets, that his Messiah* would suffer. ¹⁹Repent therefore, and turn to God so that your sins may be wiped out, ²⁰so that times of refreshing may come from the presence of the Lord, and that he may send the Messiah* appointed for you, that is, Jesus, ²¹who must remain in heaven until the time of universal restoration that God announced long ago through his holy prophets. ²²Moses said, "The Lord your God will raise up for you from your own people* a prophet like me. You must listen to whatever he tells you. ²³And it will be that everyone who does not listen to that prophet will be utterly rooted out from the people."*

> *²⁴And all the prophets, as many as have spoken, from Samuel and those after him, also predicted these days. ²⁵You are the descendants of the prophets and of the covenant that God gave to your ancestors, saying to Abraham, "And in your descendants all the families of the earth shall be blessed." ²⁶When God raised up his servant,* he sent him first to you, to bless you by turning each of you from your wicked ways.'*

Reflect

According to Peter, what was his role in the healing of the beggar?

What is the main content of Peter's message?

What does it mean to do something "in the name of Jesus"?

Respond

Be on the lookout for what Jesus wants you to do today in His name.

Encouragement: *Astonished*

Peter's second sermon in the book of Acts is prompted by a similar response as the first. In the first (on the day of Pentecost) the people were "bewildered and amazed," because each one heard the Spirit-filled followers speaking in their native language (Acts 2:6-7). In the second, the people were "utterly astonished" (Acts 3:11) at the healing of the man lame from birth.

In past readings of these texts I've missed this reaction from the people that prompts Peter's sermons. I now think it is an essential key to the movement. Formerly, I thought of the early Christian movement beginning like this:

1. The Resurrection sparks the movement.

2. The Holy Spirit ignites the flame.

3. Peter proclaims Jesus and the movement begins to spread.

But I've missed an important ingredient between 2 and 3 — the astonishment of the people who witnessed some sign that the Holy Spirit was acting (e.g. languages and healing). Before the Good News of Jesus is proclaimed, people are curious about something that has happened that they can't fit into their worldview. It is this new thing that is a sign that the new creation has burst upon the scene through the resurrection of Jesus and the coming of the Spirit. This new reality that has been given birth through the Spirit cannot be explained by the realities of the old creation; thus it must be explained by the proclamation of the new.

What will be the sign of the Holy Spirit in our lives today that might prompt curiosity and astonishment? Maybe it will be an act of healing, forgiveness or mercy. Maybe it will be a different way we treat our enemies or some boundary we cross to stand with someone that Jesus misses most. It will be this sign that prompts curiosity and openness to the Good News of how this could be possible. It is then that proclamation can spread the fire.

Blake Busick

Pray for God to reveal to you who God wants you to bless today to keep the fire of the Spirit's movement burning.

DAY 18

Begin with the prayer for guidance and discernment you wrote on Day 15.

Read Acts 4:1–22 slowly and prayerfully. What words or phrases stand out for you?

> *While Peter and John were speaking to the people, the priests, the captain of the temple, and the Sadducees came to them, ²much annoyed because they were teaching the people and proclaiming that in Jesus there is the resurrection of the dead. ³So they arrested them and put them in custody until the next day, for it was already evening. ⁴But many of those who heard the word believed; and they numbered about five thousand.*
>
> *⁵The next day their rulers, elders, and scribes assembled in Jerusalem, ⁶with Annas the high priest, Caiaphas, John, and Alexander, and all who were of the high-priestly family. ⁷When they had made the prisoners stand in their midst, they inquired, "By what power or by what name did you do this?" ⁸Then Peter, filled with the Holy Spirit, said to them, "Rulers of the people and elders, ⁹if we are questioned today because of a good deed done to someone who was sick and are asked how this man has been healed, ¹⁰let it be known to all of you, and to all the people of Israel, that this man is standing before you in good health by the name of Jesus Christ of Nazareth, whom you crucified, whom God raised from the dead. ¹¹This Jesus is 'the stone that was rejected by you, the builders; it has become the cornerstone.' ¹²There is salvation in no one else, for there is no other name under heaven given among mortals by which we must be saved." ¹³Now when they saw the boldness of Peter and John and realized that they were uneducated and ordinary men, they were amazed and recognized them as companions of Jesus. ¹⁴When they saw the man who had been cured standing beside them, they had nothing to say in opposition.*
>
> *¹⁵So they ordered them to leave the council while they discussed the matter with one another. ¹⁶They said, "What will we do with them? For it is obvious to all who live in Jerusalem that a notable sign has been done through them; we cannot deny it. ¹⁷But to keep it from spreading further among the people, let us warn them to speak no more to anyone in this name." ¹⁸So they called them and ordered them not to speak or teach at all in the name of Jesus. ¹⁹But Peter and John answered them, "Whether it is right in God's sight to listen to you rather than to God, you must judge; ²⁰for we cannot keep from speaking about what*

we have seen and heard." [21] After threatening them again, they let them go, find-ing no way to punish them because of the people, for all of them praised God for what had happened. [22] For the man on whom this sign of healing had been performed was more than forty years old.

Reflect

How do you explain the rapid number of people who came to believe?

Why did the rulers, elders and teachers resist so much?

What is your typical reaction to those who have resisted you because of your faith? Are you easily intimidated?

Respond

Practice speaking boldly about what you have seen and heard.

Encouragement: *Boldness*

I remember my college days. I was in the anti-dictatorship demonstration. Thousands and thousands of college students were in the streets. We were all of one heart. We wanted democratic government in our country, Korea. We shouted together with boldness. We were facing military tanks and rifles. Still we did not back down. "We'd rather die than to live under dictatorship!" The shout was loud enough to make the buildings shake.

In the Bible, I read the same thing. When the disciples were of one mind and one heart, they raised their voices together. They were bold. It was stated in this way: "They were all filled with the Holy Spirit and spoke the word of God with boldness." (Acts 4:31)

Today, it is hard to see "boldness" because we do not have "oneness in mind." Our culture is divided. Should we have mega churches? No, mega churches are not theologically right! So we don't pray for mega churches. Should we evangelize people and convert non-Christians into Christians? No, it is not our theology. We believe in tolerance. So, we do not pray for evangelism. Should we ask commitment and accountability from colleagues? No, we don't want to be judgmental and critical. We want to be inclusive and understanding. So we don't pray for sacrifice and commitment. Then, do we pray for small but faithful and inclusive churches? No we want to overcome financial crisis and save the institution also. So we do not pray for small but faithful and inclusive churches.

On the other hand, everybody else is united to be against churches. Herod, Pontius Pilate, with Gentiles and the people of Israel, gather together in unity against Jesus and his church! (Acts 4:27)

So, I pray that God should heal our division for us to be of one heart. I pray that God should give us one clear vision and goal of a community of love. O Lord, I pray, "Allow your miracles and wonders in our church so that we should love and respect each other and pray in one mind even when our theologies and stances are different! Have mercy on us,

O God. We are not of one heart and we are not bold! O Holy Spirit, make us members of one body, functioning differently but for one purpose of loving the world." In the name of Jesus, we pray, Amen.

Sungho Lee

Pray for those who are particularly resistant to Christ, that God would bless them and fulfill God's purpose for their lives. Pray for the Holy Spirit to keep the fire burning in the hearts of Christ's disciples everywhere.

Begin with the prayer for guidance and discernment you wrote on Day 15.

Read Acts 4:23–31 slowly and prayerfully. What words or phrases stand out for you?

> After they were released, they went to their friends and reported what the chief priests and the elders had said to them. ²⁴When they heard it, they raised their voices together to God and said, "Sovereign Lord, who made the heaven and the earth, the sea, and everything in them, ²⁵it is you who said by the Holy Spirit through our ancestor David, your servant: 'Why did the Gentiles rage, and the peoples imagine vain things? ²⁶The kings of the earth took their stand, and the rulers have gathered together against the Lord and against his Messiah.' ²⁷For in this city, in fact, both Herod and Pontius Pilate, with the Gentiles and the peoples of Israel, gathered together against your holy servant Jesus, whom you anointed, ²⁸to do whatever your hand and your plan had predestined to take place. ²⁹And now, Lord, look at their threats, and grant to your servants to speak your word with all boldness, ³⁰while you stretch out your hand to heal, and signs and wonders are performed through the name of your holy servant Jesus." ³¹When they had prayed, the place in which they were gathered together was shaken; and they were all filled with the Holy Spirit and spoke the word of God with boldness.

Reflect

What is the importance of communal prayer? What is its relationship to individual prayer?

What is the immediate result of communal prayers?

When you regularly pray with others, do you sense the presence of the Holy Spirit during those times?

Respond

Pray with some other people today in the same way these Christians prayed in today's passage.

Encouragement: *Prayer*

Today's scripture and reflection questions gave me an opportunity to reflect on my communal prayer experiences this week.

Sunday during the worship service the young people at Centennial UMC presented a moving prayer song with movement for the congregation. The young people were blessed to have learned the movements, the congregation was blessed to hear and see the good news, and together we were filled with the Holy Spirit. The word of God was spoken with boldness not only through words but also through music and the very bodies of the young people.

Yesterday I had a meeting with some of the ethnic leaders in our conference. We began with the Catch Fire in 50 days: Joining the Movement of God's Mission in the World Bible study. When we ended the study in prayer we prayed for those who are particularly resistant to Christ, that God would bless them and fulfill God's purpose for their lives; for the Holy Spirit to keep the fire burning in the hearts of Christ's disciples everywhere; and then we ended the prayer with the Lord's Prayer in our own heart languages. The very sound of our communal prayer was like music of the Kingdom of God.

Both of these experiences took place within the community of faith and involved the community in speaking the word of God in boldness.

Our study asks us to consider, "When you regularly pray with others, do you sense the presence of the Holy Spirit during those times?" My answer is YES, thanks be to God.

Linda Caldwell

Pray that God's hand would be stretched out through faith communities in your area to heal and perform miraculous signs and wonders in your neighborhood, in the name of Jesus—so that the fire keeps burning strongly.

Begin with the prayer for guidance and discernment you wrote on Day 15.

Read Acts 4:32–37 slowly and prayerfully. What words or phrases stand out for you?

> *Now the whole group of those who believed were of one heart and soul, and no one claimed private ownership of any possessions, but everything they owned was held in common. ³³With great power the apostles gave their testimony to the resurrection of the Lord Jesus, and great grace was upon them all. ³⁴There was not a needy person among them, for as many as owned lands or houses sold them and brought the proceeds of what was sold. ³⁵They laid it at the apostles' feet, and it was distributed to each as any had need. ³⁶There was a Levite, a native of Cyprus, Joseph, to whom the apostles gave the name Barnabas (which means 'son of encouragement'). ³⁷He sold a field that belonged to him, then brought the money, and laid it at the apostles' feet.*

Reflect

Are you of one heart and mind with other believers?

What is the relationship between being filled with the Holy Spirit and the believers' unity, sharing of possessions and powerful testimony?

How might you express your generosity more extravagantly?

Respond

> Do one simple thing that brings your faith community a step closer to being of "one heart and soul."

> OR

> Demonstrate your extravagant generosity today.

Encouragement: *All You Need Is Love*

> The currency in the early church was love, not money, not property. Their hearts were so filled with love that they could be thought of as having "one heart and soul." Take a deep breath and remember the last time your heart was filled with love. Remember how any fear or pain lost its grip? Exhale.

> As Christians we claim access to that eternal love. Our first and second commandments are to practice it. Sometimes we wrestle with it till the break of day. It is infinite, it is ours, and we must call it into our life together.

> *Diane Knudsen*

Pray for our churches to move more confidently to a place where we are operating out of one heart and soul and where everything we "own" is held in common and used for God's purposes. For this unity and common trust to fuel the Holy Spirit fire burning across our nation.

Begin with the prayer for guidance and discernment you wrote on Day 15.

Read 1 Peter 1:13–25 slowly and prayerfully. What words or phrases stand out for you?

> [13]Therefore prepare your minds for action; discipline yourselves; set all your hope on the grace that Jesus Christ will bring you when he is revealed. [14]Like obedient children, do not be conformed to the desires that you formerly had in ignorance. [15]Instead, as he who called you is holy, be holy yourselves in all your conduct; [16]for it is written, 'You shall be holy, for I am holy.'
>
> [17]If you invoke as Father the one who judges all people impartially according to their deeds, live in reverent fear during the time of your exile. [18]You know that you were ransomed from the futile ways inherited from your ancestors, not with perishable things like silver or gold, [19]but with the precious blood of Christ, like that of a lamb without defect or blemish. [20]He was destined before the foundation of the world, but was revealed at the end of the ages for your sake. [21]Through him you have come to trust in God, who raised him from the dead and gave him glory, so that your faith and hope are set on God.
>
> [22]Now that you have purified your souls by your obedience to the truth so that you have genuine mutual love, love one another deeply from the heart. [23]You have been born anew, not of perishable but of imperishable seed, through the living and enduring word of God. [24]For
>
> > 'All flesh is like grass
> > and all its glory like the flower of grass.
> > The grass withers,
> > and the flower falls,
> > [25]but the word of the Lord endures for ever.'
>
> That word is the good news that was announced to you.

Reflect

What does it mean to be holy?

What is the relationship between being purified and love?

How genuine and deep is your love for others in your church?

Respond

Make one adjustment in your thinking and behavior that allows you to be more disciplined and hopeful as described in verse 13.

Encouragement: *Whisperings*

Do you hear the whisperings of the Holy Spirit? Do you heed them?

Usually I hesitate — and then it's too late.

Yesterday my friend and I were leaving the place where we'd had lunch. I spotted the dog first, then the young man sitting beside her under a tree. The dog looked peaceful, basking in the leaf-filtered sunlight, but the boy did not. He looked sad as he turned toward me, evidently having sensed my eyes on him. Homeless, I thought. A cardboard sign seemed to have been discarded as though the boy had lost all hope that anyone would help.

The Spirit told me to turn off the engine and walk over to the young man, but I drove away instead. My friend was telling a story and to interrupt seemed ridiculous.

But the Spirit persisted. Instead of heading to work I turned back into the parking lot, and parked again. I approached the boy.

"Are you alright?" I asked. We talked for a few minutes. He was only 21, and hitchhiking to Washington with his girlfriend and his dog. In the summer, he said, they were going south to work at a carnival. I liked him.

I asked him if he had money. He didn't, so I gave him some. I told him to be careful, to watch out when they accepted rides. The encounter was out of character for me, yet strangely seemed quite natural, like talking to my own son.

I like to think we parted as friends. His face will stay with me for awhile.

Yesterday the Spirit spoke to me, and for once I listened. For once I obeyed. And I know which one of us was blessed.

I am in awe.

Cate Monaghan

Pray for strength to be obedient to the truth so that you have genuine mutual love—loving others deeply from the heart—which enables loving, Christ-like action in your church and community and keeps the fire burning

Week 4

Jesus came that we might have life that is rich and overflowing (John). This abundant life is like a fire that shines brightly or all to see. Against pressure from without and challenges from within (Acts) it glows and many are attracted to it. As our spiritual intensity deepens, our missional alignment translates into dynamic relationships that overcome obstacles and limitations.

Christ has made us a new people. Remember who you are (First Peter).

We were laughing, telling stories and drinking espresso,
lingering at our dinner table, all of us bathed in moonlight,
on the shore of the Sea of Galilee. Pointing upward, I asked
my hosts, 'Tell me — What city is that sparkling on top of
that mountain?' I thought it a bit odd, since cities usually
grow up in valleys. My hosts replied, "Oh, that is Safed."
And a chill ran up my spine, for I knew the story of Safed: a
city older than Jesus. And then I zoned away momentarily
into a holy place, apart from the stories and the espresso,
to marvel at the witness of such a town, clinging to the top
of the mountain by its claws, shining faithfully up there.
Shining for so many centuries back across time that
Jesus certainly saw it as he taught his disciples in roughly
the place where we dined, saying to them (and to us):
'A city set on hill cannot be hidden.'

Paul Nixon,
reflecting on a trip to Israel in 1998.

This little light of mine, I'm gonna let it shine.

This little light of mine, I'm gonna let it shine,
let it shine, let it shine, let it shine.

19th century American folk song

Catch Fire in 50 Days

Pray for guidance and discernment. If you wish, write that prayer here and use it for the next six days.

Read John 10:1–10 slowly and prayerfully. What words or phrases stand out for you?

> 'Very truly, I tell you, anyone who does not enter the sheepfold by the gate but climbs in by another way is a thief and a bandit. ²The one who enters by the gate is the shepherd of the sheep. ³The gatekeeper opens the gate for him, and the sheep hear his voice. He calls his own sheep by name and leads them out. ⁴When he has brought out all his own, he goes ahead of them, and the sheep follow him because they know his voice. ⁵They will not follow a stranger, but they will run from him because they do not know the voice of strangers.' ⁶Jesus used this figure of speech with them, but they did not understand what he was saying to them.
>
> ⁷So again Jesus said to them, 'Very truly, I tell you, I am the gate for the sheep. ⁸All who came before me are thieves and bandits; but the sheep did not listen to them. ⁹I am the gate. Whoever enters by me will be saved, and will come in and go out and find pasture. ¹⁰The thief comes only to steal and kill and destroy. I came that they may have life, and have it abundantly.

Reflect

How do you continue to hear and follow the voice of Jesus amidst all the competing noise in the world?

How would you describe the abundant life Jesus is talking about?

On a scale of 1-10 (10 being the highest), how abundant is your life right now?

Respond

Listen for and do one thing that will increase your connection to Jesus and the abundance He offers.

Encouragement: *Abundant Life*

Today's "Catch Fire" question asks: "On a scale of 1-10, how abundant is your life right now?"

"Well," I might answer, "that depends…"

…that depends on if I compare myself to my highly gifted, talented, "well-heeled" neighbor to my right, or if I compare myself to my needy, seedy, greedy neighbor to my left. Looking to my right, I could realize what I don't have and feel slighted. And looking to my left, I could realize how bad others have it and feel elevated, better than and more blessed than my neighbor.

…that depends on if I find that I must compare and contrast myself to others in order to realize my abundance, my blessings.

…that depends on if I must put myself down or put another person, community, or nation down to realize who has abundant life.

…that depends on if, instead, I might be one who depends on the Giver of abundant life for that very greatest of blessings. And if this is where my dependence is found, then, my answer to today's question is: yes. Yes. YES!

Mariellen Yoshino

Pray for discernment about how God might want to use you to shine more brightly on the Gatekeeper of Abundant Life. To shine in ways which will lead more people—your friends, family, co-workers, colleagues, acquaintances, etc.—to Jesus.

Begin with the prayer for guidance and discernment you wrote on Day 22.

Read Acts 5:1–11 slowly and prayerfully. What words or phrases stand out for you?

> But a man named Ananias, with the consent of his wife Sapphira, sold a piece of property; ²with his wife's knowledge, he kept back some of the proceeds, and brought only a part and laid it at the apostles' feet. ³'Ananias,' Peter asked, 'why has Satan filled your heart to lie to the Holy Spirit and to keep back part of the proceeds of the land? ⁴While it remained unsold, did it not remain your own? And after it was sold, were not the proceeds at your disposal? How is it that you have contrived this deed in your heart? You did not lie to us but to God!' ⁵Now when Ananias heard these words, he fell down and died. And great fear seized all who heard of it. ⁶The young men came and wrapped up his body, then carried him out and buried him.
>
> ⁷After an interval of about three hours his wife came in, not knowing what had happened. ⁸Peter said to her, 'Tell me whether you and your husband sold the land for such and such a price.' And she said, 'Yes, that was the price.' ⁹Then Peter said to her, 'How is it that you have agreed together to put the Spirit of the Lord to the test? Look, the feet of those who have buried your husband are at the door, and they will carry you out.' ¹⁰Immediately she fell down at his feet and died. When the young men came in they found her dead, so they carried her out and buried her beside her husband. ¹¹And great fear seized the whole church and all who heard of these things.

Reflect

Why is this story included at this point in the story of the early Church?

What's the big deal?

How transparent and truthful are you when it comes to your participation in church?

Respond

Identify an area of your life that needs to be more transparent and truthful so that God is clearly more central. Do one thing today that can move you in that direction.

Encouragement: *No 'Plan B'*

Today's reading, Acts 5:1-11, is the sermon illustration for Acts 4:32-37. In the fourth chapter of Acts we have this nice picture of believers who were joyfully bringing all that they had, so that there was not a needy person among them. It's all good.

Then we move into the fifth chapter of Acts and the story of the power of sharing takes a rather dark turn. Ananias and Sapphira thought that they could beat the system. Give some, and hold back some. Who would know? What would it hurt?

As Disciples of Jesus Christ there is no holding back, no plan B, and no room for turning your back on those with whom you journey in faith. Every time we hold back and pretend to participate in the full mission of the church a piece of us dies. This is true for individuals and for entire congregations.

It is very hard to fully live an abundant life in Christ when your hands are full of the things you will not share. This holding on limits your capacity to take in the Holy Spirit and it limits your capacity to reach out in love to others.

Linda Caldwell

Pray for the Spirit to guide your every action so that you might shine forth God's truths more brightly.

Begin with the prayer for guidance and discernment you wrote on Day 22.

Read Acts 5:12–16 slowly and prayerfully. What words or phrases stand out for you?

> Now many signs and wonders were done among the people through the apostles. And they were all together in Solomon's Portico. 13None of the rest dared to join them, but the people held them in high esteem. *14Yet more than ever believers were added to the Lord, great numbers of both men and women, 15so that they even carried out the sick into the streets, and laid them on cots and mats, in order that Peter's shadow might fall on some of them as he came by. 16A great number of people would also gather from the towns around Jerusalem, bringing the sick and those tormented by unclean spirits, and they were all cured.*

Reflect

What is the last sign and wonder you have witnessed: In your life? In your faith community?

Why were believers being added more than ever?

How might you and your congregation better position yourselves to be instruments of God's healing?

Respond

Engage in an act of healing with Holy Spirit power and alleviate someone's suffering today.

Encouragement: *Signs and Wonders*

I've been noticing the connection between "signs and wonders" and people being "added to the Lord." These wonders are signs that the Holy Spirit is working through the believers. One day it is the ability to communicate the Gospel in different languages, another day it is healing. What is shining brightly through the followers of Jesus is the light (or fire) of the Holy Spirit.

If we are to add great numbers to the Lord there must be evidence that the Holy Spirit is working through our lives. We can see these not only in acts of communication and healing but also in acts of forgiveness, extravagant generosity, love of enemies and other ways we bear witness that we are living in a new creation. These acts can't be explained by the old order. They can only be explained by a proclamation that Christ is risen and we are filled with the light of the Holy Spirit shining brightly through us.

What sign or wonder might the Holy Spirit shine through us today?

Blake Busick

Pray that God might bring someone into your life today who needs some kind of healing or relief from suffering. Pray for the courage and insight to respond so that the healing power of the Holy Spirit shines more brightly.

Begin with the prayer for guidance and discernment you wrote on Day 22.

Read Acts 5:17–42 slowly and prayerfully. What words or phrases stand out for you?

> Then the high priest took action; he and all who were with him (that is, the sect of the Sadducees), being filled with jealousy, 18arrested the apostles and put them in the public prison. ¹⁹But during the night an angel of the Lord opened the prison doors, brought them out, and said, ²⁰'Go, stand in the temple and tell the people the whole message about this life.' ²¹When they heard this, they entered the temple at daybreak and went on with their teaching.
>
> When the high priest and those with him arrived, they called together the council and the whole body of the elders of Israel, and sent to the prison to have them brought. ²²But when the temple police went there, they did not find them in the prison; so they returned and reported, ²³'We found the prison securely locked and the guards standing at the doors, but when we opened them, we found no one inside.' ²⁴Now when the captain of the temple and the chief priests heard these words, they were perplexed about them, wondering what might be going on. ²⁵Then someone arrived and announced, 'Look, the men whom you put in prison are standing in the temple and teaching the people!' ²⁶Then the captain went with the temple police and brought them, but without violence, for they were afraid of being stoned by the people.
>
> ²⁷When they had brought them, they had them stand before the council. The high priest questioned them, ²⁸saying, 'We gave you strict orders not to teach in this name, yet here you have filled Jerusalem with your teaching and you are determined to bring this man's blood on us.' ²⁹But Peter and the apostles answered, 'We must obey God rather than any human authority. ³⁰The God of our ancestors raised up Jesus, whom you had killed by hanging him on a tree. ³¹God exalted him at his right hand as Leader and Saviour, so that he might give repentance to Israel and forgiveness of sins. ³²And we are witnesses to these things, and so is the Holy Spirit whom God has given to those who obey him.'
>
> ³³When they heard this, they were enraged and wanted to kill them. ³⁴But a Pharisee in the council named Gamaliel, a teacher of the law, respected by all the people, stood up and ordered the men to be put outside for a short time.

35Then he said to them, 'Fellow-Israelites, consider carefully what you propose to do to these men. 36For some time ago Theudas rose up, claiming to be somebody, and a number of men, about four hundred, joined him; but he was killed, and all who followed him were dispersed and disappeared. 37After him Judas the Galilean rose up at the time of the census and got people to follow him; he also perished, and all who followed him were scattered. 38So in the present case, I tell you, keep away from these men and let them alone; because if this plan or this undertaking is of human origin, it will fail; 39but if it is of God, you will not be able to overthrow them—in that case you may even be found fighting against God!'

They were convinced by him, 40and when they had called in the apostles, they had them flogged. Then they ordered them not to speak in the name of Jesus, and let them go. 41As they left the council, they rejoiced that they were considered worthy to suffer dishonour for the sake of the name. 42And every day in the temple and at home they did not cease to teach and proclaim Jesus as the Messiah.

Reflect

When is the last time you experienced opposition for making learners and followers of Jesus?

What tension are you experiencing between obeying God versus obeying human authority?

What plans in your life or in the life of your congregation are your own? What plans are of God?

Respond

Change one of your plans (personal or congregational) for God's plans.

Encouragement: *Not a Great Action Movie*

This story seems so authentic and refreshing. First, the apostles were so brave and straightforward in telling the authorities their experience of Jesus. Then the authorities had a person in their midst who was respected by all people. And that person was wise and not afraid to acknowledge the possibility that God was really at work. And the people listened to him. Then, they showed some mercy toward the apostles when they could've gotten very defensive and killed them on the spot.

This would not make for a great action movie. Nobody is getting Rambo'd up.

This drama replays all the time in human affairs. Sooner or later we all have the opportunity to play the part of Gamaliel, to remind the angry crowd that maybe we should step back and consider the possibility that God is up to something here. And God is always up to something.

Diane Knudsen

Pray for the boldness to shine brightly as a witness for Christ through your words and deeds. Give thanks no matter what reaction your testimony sparks.

Begin with the prayer for guidance and discernment you wrote on Day 22.

Read Acts 6:1–7 slowly and prayerfully. What words or phrases stand out for you?

> *Now during those days, when the disciples were increasing in number, the Hellenists complained against the Hebrews because their widows were being neglected in the daily distribution of food. ²And the twelve called together the whole community of the disciples and said, 'It is not right that we should neglect the word of God in order to wait at tables. ³Therefore, friends, select from among yourselves seven men of good standing, full of the Spirit and of wisdom, whom we may appoint to this task, ⁴while we, for our part, will devote ourselves to prayer and to serving the word.' ⁵What they said pleased the whole community, and they chose Stephen, a man full of faith and the Holy Spirit, together with Philip, Prochorus, Nicanor, Timon, Parmenas, and Nicolaus, a proselyte of Antioch. ⁶They had these men stand before the apostles, who prayed and laid their hands on them.*

Reflect

How do you account for the word of God continuing to spread? How is this first century context like and unlike our own?

How well is your church organized so that the Word of God, practical tasks and ministry are all lived out and led appropriately?

By what criteria do you select and support leaders in your church?

Respond

If you are **not** actively serving in your faith community, get connected in an area which matches your spiritual gifts and passions.

If you **are** actively serving in your faith community, ask for feedback so that you are certain that you are serving in the right place given your giftedness and passions.

Encouragement: *From Complaints to Blessings*

Sometimes when I visit with church leaders, a striking image comes to mind. Often we are sitting at some sort of table, perhaps one of those standard 8-foot folding tables that we move around our fellowship halls. Or perhaps our chairs are gathered around a fancier wood table that has been the center of church planning and decisions for many years in that particular congregation.

At times our conversations are hard, with complaints on how a program is going or whether a pastor ought to lead in a particular way. Some of us Christians get very passionate in sharing our concerns, don't we?

And at that moment, I imagine painting the whole table with grace. Pouring it over freely and letting it drip into our conversations. It is not just a moment of dreaming. It is a moment of holy affirmation, because I know it is true. God is, at every minute, painting the whole table, the whole room, our whole hearts with grace.

With grace flowing, we might remember how the Gospel is growing our church, perhaps, in spite of our complaining… just as in the church described in our passage. With grace, we would realize that our serving at tables was a way of serving the Word, of praying with our hands. With grace at the table, we see God's work of possibility, even in difficult times.

In the end on that day in the ancient church, grace did its grace-full work, and seven men of faith were chosen for the holy work of service to the widows. And the disciples offered a blessing.

May we receive and share the grace with abundance as we live in these in-between times of possibility in our lives and our congregations.

Kristie Olah

Pray to be so full of faith and the Holy Spirit that you can't help but shine brightly. In that Spirit, pray that you would gracefully provide spiritual leadership to your congregation and the world.

Begin with the prayer for guidance and discernment you wrote on Day 22.

Read Acts 6:8–15 slowly and prayerfully. What words or phrases stand out for you?

> Stephen, full of grace and power, did great wonders and signs among the people. ⁹Then some of those who belonged to the synagogue of the Freedmen (as it was called), Cyrenians, Alexandrians, and others of those from Cilicia and Asia, stood up and argued with Stephen. ¹⁰But they could not withstand the wisdom and the Spirit with which he spoke. ¹¹Then they secretly instigated some men to say, 'We have heard him speak blasphemous words against Moses and God.' ¹²They stirred up the people as well as the elders and the scribes; then they suddenly confronted him, seized him, and brought him before the council. ¹³They set up false witnesses who said, 'This man never stops saying things against this holy place and the law; ¹⁴for we have heard him say that this Jesus of Nazareth will destroy this place and will change the customs that Moses handed on to us.' ¹⁵And all who sat in the council looked intently at him, and they saw that his face was like the face of an angel.

Reflect

Stephen is described as being full of grace and power. Would anyone describe you this way?

What great wonders and signs might God want to do through you?

Have you ever been a false witness or instigated another person to be one? Has anyone ever brought a false testimony against you?

Respond

Take steps to correct any past actions you've taken (i.e., false witness or instigation), or forgive those who have falsely accused you. Do this with grace and power.

Encouragement: *Angel*

So what does the "face of an angel" look like?

Curly hair, chubby cheeks? Does the angel aim an arrow on Valentine's Day?

Is it the hardened warrior of God? Michael bringing vengeance?

Is it the wondering and worried look of a Gabriel telling a girl what she cannot understand, and hearing her consent to what she cannot know?

I was told an angel is a messenger.

I hear the message from one who knows and loves me.

Grace and power come from compassion, I think (and hope!).

Perhaps the face of an angel is the face of a friend who tells the truth.

I pray that, from time to time, it is my face for others.

Ted Virts

Pray for those who are facing tough opposition or persecution because of their faith—that the power and grace of the Spirit might shine brightly.

Begin with the prayer for guidance and discernment you wrote on Day 22.

Read 1 Peter 2:1–10 slowly and prayerfully. What words or phrases stand out for you?

> Rid yourselves, therefore, of all malice, and all guile, insincerity, envy, and all slander. [2]Like newborn infants, long for the pure, spiritual milk, so that by it you may grow into salvation—[3]if indeed you have tasted that the Lord is good.
>
> [4]Come to him, a living stone, though rejected by mortals yet chosen and precious in God's sight, and [5]like living stones, let yourselves be built into a spiritual house, to be a holy priesthood, to offer spiritual sacrifices acceptable to God through Jesus Christ. [6]For it stands in scripture:
>
> > 'See, I am laying in Zion a stone,
> >   a cornerstone chosen and precious;
> > and whoever believes in him
> >   will not be put to shame.'
>
> [7]To you then who believe, he is precious; but for those who do not believe,
> >   'The stone that the builders rejected
> >   has become the very head of the corner',
>
> [8]and
> >   'A stone that makes them stumble,
> >   and a rock that makes them fall.'
>
> They stumble because they disobey the word, as they were destined to do.
>
> [9]But you are a chosen race, a royal priesthood, a holy nation, God's own people, in order that you may proclaim the mighty acts of him who called you out of darkness into his marvelous light.
>
> > [10]Once you were not a people,
> >   but now you are God's people;
> > once you had not received mercy,
> >   but now you have received mercy.

Reflect

What do you need to rid yourself of so that you can grow into your salvation?

What would change if each member of your faith community were viewed as "living stones built into a spiritual house"?

What does it mean that you are a holy (or royal) priesthood?

Respond

As a holy priesthood, spend several moments today interceding for the world.

Encouragement: *God's People*

For me, this is a reminder that an overarching theme is encouragement to Christians who are suffering or are about to suffer persecution, reminding us all of the source of our identity as God's people and a responsibility to live out that identity in the midst of pain and suffering. Faithfulness in actions and union as a community then are to be the mark of God's people. Even when we feel alienated from much in our life journey, we have been reborn as children of God, and are therefore members of God's household.

Jerry Smith

Pray that God would shine brightly in the world through God's holy priesthood and that more living stones would be added to spiritual houses throughout our nation.

Week 5

Jesus has made it possible for us not only to do His works, but to do even greater works. All we need to do is ask in His name (John). The preaching and martyrdom of Stephen and the subsequent spread of the gospel to Samaria are evidence of this potential. Christ is our example of how to respond to those who do us wrong as we carry out the mission of God (First Peter).

As you enter the last three weeks of this discernment, please pay special attention to the restlessness that God might be stirring in you. Share any nudges or odd thoughts with two or three others in your congregation.

Sometimes to fan the flame we need to add oxygen or space between the logs. Take a day off to do nothing but to rest in God.

Someday, after mastering the winds, the waves, the tides and gravity, we shall harness for God the energies of love, and then, for a second time in the history of the world, we will have discovered fire.

Pierre Teilhard de Chardin,
20th Century French Paleontologist

Pray for guidance and discernment. If you wish, write that prayer here and use it for the next six days.

Read John 14:1–14 slowly and prayerfully. What words or phrases stand out for you?

> 'Do not let your hearts be troubled. Believe in God, believe also in me. [2]In my Father's house there are many dwelling-places. If it were not so, would I have told you that I go to prepare a place for you? [3]And if I go and prepare a place for you, I will come again and will take you to myself, so that where I am, there you may be also. [4]And you know the way to the place where I am going.' [5]Thomas said to him, 'Lord, we do not know where you are going. How can we know the way?' [6]Jesus said to him, 'I am the way, and the truth, and the life. No one comes to the Father except through me. [7]If you know me, you will know my Father also. From now on you do know him and have seen him.'

> [8]Philip said to him, 'Lord, show us the Father, and we will be satisfied.' [9]Jesus said to him, 'Have I been with you all this time, Philip, and you still do not know me? Whoever has seen me has seen the Father. How can you say, "Show us the Father"? [10]Do you not believe that I am in the Father and the Father is in me? The words that I say to you I do not speak on my own; but the Father who dwells in me does his works. [11]Believe me that I am in the Father and the Father is in me; but if you do not, then believe me because of the works themselves. [12]Very truly, I tell you, the one who believes in me will also do the works that I do and, in fact, will do greater works than these, because I am going to the Father. [13]I will do whatever you ask in my name, so that the Father may be glorified in the Son. [14]If in my name you ask me for anything, I will do it.

Reflect

> Is your heart troubled about anything? How can you find reassurance in the words of Jesus?

What will it take for you to be satisfied with your beliefs (v. 8)? How are you continuing to seek reassurance in the promises of Jesus?

How might verses 12-14 help you fan the flame of your faith and that of those around you?

Respond

Discern God's will about some area of your life, faith community or work. Ask boldly, in the name of Christ, that it be done in a way which might fan the flame of God's missional movement in the world.

Encouragement: *WWJD?*

I have read this passage from the Gospel of John countless times for funeral and memorial services. I am comforted by it, as are those attending the service. Reading it now as a part of the study gives me an opportunity to see it in a different light.

Today I am struck by verses 12–14. Can it really be that disciples of Jesus, ones who believe, are able to impact the world as Jesus did? It casts a new light on the WWJD? (What Would Jesus Do?) bracelets. It seems worth it to ask the question. We are told: "the one who believes in me will also do the works that I do…" In light of this passage, asking the question — "What Would Jesus Do?" becomes more than some editorial question put out to the universe. It is a reminder to followers of Jesus to act in a way that will demonstrate the love of Jesus through our actions in Jesus' name.

I think John Wesley might have had a use for a WWJD bracelet. He believed verse 12 in our reading: "Very truly I tell you, the one who believes in me will also do the works that I do and, in fact, will do greater works than these because I am going to the father." Wesley called for a holiness of heart and life. He saw the possibility of having a heart so all-flaming with the love of God that it would be continually offering up every thought, word, and work as a spiritual sacrifice, acceptable to God through Christ.

On this day I am thankful for the very powerful reminder that all is possible through him who loved us and that we are called not to just celebrate that fact but to act on our belief as well.

Linda Caldwell

Pray for the Holy Spirit to fan the flame of faith and belief in someone whose heart is troubled or in someone whose mind is still searching for evidence of Jesus in our midst.

Begin with the prayer for guidance and discernment you wrote on Day 29.

Read Acts 7:1–53 slowly and prayerfully. What words or phrases stand out for you?

> Then the high priest asked him, 'Are these things so?' ²And Stephen replied:

> 'Brothers and fathers, listen to me. The God of glory appeared to our ancestor Abraham when he was in Mesopotamia, before he lived in Haran, ³and said to him, "Leave your country and your relatives and go to the land that I will show you." ⁴Then he left the country of the Chaldeans and settled in Haran. After his father died, God had him move from there to this country in which you are now living. ⁵He did not give him any of it as a heritage, not even a foot's length, but promised to give it to him as his possession and to his descendants after him, even though he had no child. ⁶And God spoke in these terms, that his descendants would be resident aliens in a country belonging to others, who would enslave them and maltreat them for four hundred years. ⁷"But I will judge the nation that they serve," said God, "and after that they shall come out and worship me in this place." ⁸Then he gave him the covenant of circumcision. And so Abraham became the father of Isaac and circumcised him on the eighth day; and Isaac became the father of Jacob, and Jacob of the twelve patriarchs.

> ⁹'The patriarchs, jealous of Joseph, sold him into Egypt; but God was with him, ¹⁰and rescued him from all his afflictions, and enabled him to win favor and to show wisdom when he stood before Pharaoh, king of Egypt, who appointed him ruler over Egypt and over all his household. ¹¹Now there came a famine throughout Egypt and Canaan, and great suffering, and our ancestors could find no food. ¹²But when Jacob heard that there was grain in Egypt, he sent our ancestors there on their first visit. ¹³On the second visit Joseph made himself known to his brothers, and Joseph's family became known to Pharaoh. ¹⁴Then Joseph sent and invited his father Jacob and all his relatives to come to him, seventy-five in all; ¹⁵so Jacob went down to Egypt. He himself died there as well as our ancestors, ¹⁶and their bodies were brought back to Shechem and laid in the tomb that Abraham had bought for a sum of silver from the sons of Hamor in Shechem.

> ¹⁷'But as the time drew near for the fulfillment of the promise that God had made to Abraham, our people in Egypt increased and multiplied ¹⁸until

another king who had not known Joseph ruled over Egypt. ¹⁹He dealt craftily with our race and forced our ancestors to abandon their infants so that they would die. ²⁰At this time Moses was born, and he was beautiful before God. For three months he was brought up in his father's house; ²¹and when he was abandoned, Pharaoh's daughter adopted him and brought him up as her own son. ²²So Moses was instructed in all the wisdom of the Egyptians and was powerful in his words and deeds.

²³'When he was forty years old, it came into his heart to visit his relatives, the Israelites. ²⁴When he saw one of them being wronged, he defended the oppressed man and avenged him by striking down the Egyptian. ²⁵He supposed that his kinsfolk would understand that God through him was rescuing them, but they did not understand. ²⁶The next day he came to some of them as they were quarrelling and tried to reconcile them, saying, "Men, you are brothers; why do you wrong each other?" ²⁷But the man who was wronging his neighbor pushed Moses aside, saying, "Who made you a ruler and a judge over us? ²⁸Do you want to kill me as you killed the Egyptian yesterday?" ²⁹When he heard this, Moses fled and became a resident alien in the land of Midian. There he became the father of two sons.

³⁰'Now when forty years had passed, an angel appeared to him in the wilderness of Mount Sinai, in the flame of a burning bush. ³¹When Moses saw it, he was amazed at the sight; and as he approached to look, there came the voice of the Lord: ³²"I am the God of your ancestors, the God of Abraham, Isaac, and Jacob." Moses began to tremble and did not dare to look. ³³Then the Lord said to him, "Take off the sandals from your feet, for the place where you are standing is holy ground. ³⁴I have surely seen the mistreatment of my people who are in Egypt and have heard their groaning, and I have come down to rescue them. Come now, I will send you to Egypt."

³⁵'It was this Moses whom they rejected when they said, "Who made you a ruler and a judge?" and whom God now sent as both ruler and liberator through the angel who appeared to him in the bush. ³⁶He led them out, having performed wonders and signs in Egypt, at the Red Sea, and in the wilderness for forty years. ³⁷This is the Moses who said to the Israelites, "God will raise up a prophet for you from your own people as he raised me up." ³⁸He is the one who was in the

congregation in the wilderness with the angel who spoke to him at Mount Sinai, and with our ancestors; and he received living oracles to give to us. ³⁹Our ancestors were unwilling to obey him; instead, they pushed him aside, and in their hearts they turned back to Egypt, ⁴⁰saying to Aaron, "Make gods for us who will lead the way for us; as for this Moses who led us out from the land of Egypt, we do not know what has happened to him." ⁴¹At that time they made a calf, offered a sacrifice to the idol, and revelled in the works of their hands. ⁴²But God turned away from them and handed them over to worship the host of heaven, as it is written in the book of the prophets:

> "Did you offer to me slain victims and sacrifices
>> for forty years in the wilderness, O house of Israel?
> ⁴³No; you took along the tent of Moloch,
>> and the star of your god Rephan,
>> the images that you made to worship;
> so I will remove you beyond Babylon."

⁴⁴'Our ancestors had the tent of testimony in the wilderness, as God directed when he spoke to Moses, ordering him to make it according to the pattern he had seen. ⁴⁵Our ancestors in turn brought it in with Joshua when they dispossessed the nations that God drove out before our ancestors. And it was there until the time of David, ⁴⁶who found favour with God and asked that he might find a dwelling-place for the house of Jacob. ⁴⁷But it was Solomon who built a house for him. ⁴⁸Yet the Most High does not dwell in houses made by human hands; as the prophet says,

> ⁴⁹"Heaven is my throne,
>> and the earth is my footstool.
> What kind of house will you build for me, says the Lord,
>> or what is the place of my rest?
> ⁵⁰Did not my hand make all these things?"

⁵¹'You stiff-necked people, uncircumcised in heart and ears, you are for ever opposing the Holy Spirit, just as your ancestors used to do. ⁵²Which of the prophets did your ancestors not persecute? They killed those who foretold the coming of the Righteous One, and now you have become his betrayers and murderers.

[53]*You are the ones that received the law as ordained by angels, and yet you have not kept it.'*

Reflect

Why does Stephen rehearse a history that his hearers already know?

As you read Stephen's speech, what part of it feels most relevant to you? To your faith community's context?

What would you need to do in order to become more open to the Holy Spirit?

Respond

Open yourself to receive instruction and intercession by the Holy Spirit today.

Encouragement: *Can We Be the Church of the Future?*

Today's reading talks of "stiff-necked" people opposing the Holy Spirit. What came to me was the many discussions I've had with youth workers, around the frustrations they sometimes have in their ministry because their opposition comes in the phrase, "but we've always done it…." As we as the Church look to be open to the Holy Spirit to help us "catch fire," we cannot be limited by what is known, what is comfortable, and what might have worked in the past — in visioning the Church of the future.

I was listening to NPR and it was talking about the floods in Memphis and how during this crisis, emergency outreach and support was very different. It was the local churches which were the leaders in providing support and aid to the victims of the flood. In fact, if one were to go to the Red Cross, that person would be referred to the churches as the "primary" support and contact agency during this disaster. The Red Cross spokesperson said this was an unprecedented procedure. The way it had "always been done" was that the Red Cross would be the lead agency and reach out to the churches to support Red Cross efforts. The spokesperson of the organized church community stated, "We knew our place and purpose in this time, and took action as Christians to move and act as we are called to do."

This struck me as a powerful shift in allowing the Holy Spirit to work among them and to call and send them to act, regardless of what "had always" been done in the past. Through their willingness to be open to the Holy Spirit, they not only served those in need, but were a witness of God's grace and compassion to all.

So…can we answer the call to be the "Church of the Now" rather than "stiff-necked," and stuck in what we have "always done"…?

Kelly Newell

Pray for the people of all churches and faith communities, that we would not be a "stiff-necked" people," but rather would join the movement of the Holy Spirit in a way which fans the flame.

Begin with the prayer for guidance and discernment you wrote on Day 29.

Read Acts 7:54–60 slowly and prayerfully. What words or phrases stand out for you?

> When they heard these things, they became enraged and ground their teeth at Stephen. *55But filled with the Holy Spirit, he gazed into heaven and saw the glory of God and Jesus standing at the right hand of God. 56'Look,' he said, 'I see the heavens opened and the Son of Man standing at the right hand of God!' 57But they covered their ears, and with a loud shout all rushed together against him. 58Then they dragged him out of the city and began to stone him; and the witnesses laid their coats at the feet of a young man named Saul. 59While they were stoning Stephen, he prayed, 'Lord Jesus, receive my spirit.' 60Then he knelt down and cried out in a loud voice, 'Lord, do not hold this sin against them.' When he had said this, he died.*

Reflect

Why was the resistance to Stephen so intense?

What are the similarities and differences between Stephen's death and Jesus'?

What role does persecution play in fanning the flame?

Respond

Journal about your experiences of:
1. being the person persecuted;
2. being the one throwing stones (stones may take the form of gossip, ridicule, or more public/obvious forms);
3. being on the sidelines watching someone who boldly proclaimed the word of God being brought down or strongly challenged.

Read what you wrote and ask God for a next step.

Encouragement: 'Phil's Choice'

Stephen sets the bar for us second only to Jesus himself. Could I take the stand he did? He surely knew what would happen. How many times have I stepped out to proclaim my faith in some way, knowing it would cost me? How many times did I fail to state my faith? I don't live where this type of scenario would cost me my life, but the news media tells me this situation does exist today — in places such as Sudan, Egypt, Iraq, and the Philippines.

I am reminded of the question, "If it were a criminal offence to be a Christian, would there be enough evidence to convict me?" I hope the answer would be yes. But the real question is still out there: If it would cost me my life, would I take the stand of Stephen?

If I don't see myself as a martyr, do I see myself as a passive bystander? I hope that would not be the case. Could I pick up a stone and hurl it? I am haunted by those questions. I pray that as the days go by, I will remember the story of Stephen and choose his role over that of the others there that day.

Phil Bandy

Pray that you might forgive those who sin against you and that your congregation might fan the flame of God's mission by standing up for those who speak out or act as Christ in their context.

Begin with the prayer for guidance and discernment you wrote on Day 29.

Read Acts 8:1–3 slowly and prayerfully. What words or phrases stand out for you?

> *And Saul approved of their killing him.*
>
> *That day a severe persecution began against the church in Jerusalem, and all except the apostles were scattered throughout the countryside of Judea and Samaria. ²Devout men buried Stephen and made loud lamentation over him. ³But Saul was ravaging the church by entering house after house; dragging off both men and women, he committed them to prison.*

Reflect

When has God taken something negative in your life and used it for good?

What will be the effect of the scattering of the early followers of Jesus?

What prison do you find yourself in today?

Respond

Identify how your prison experience might prepare you to be a better witness for Christ.

Encouragement: *A Turning Point in My Faith Journey*

Wow, this is the first time I have ever read these three verses without reading the story that precedes and the story that follows them. I have always looked at this as a transition, in which the death of Stephen is the beginning of Saul, which ultimately takes us to Paul and his ministry. But to read it as a stand-alone reading? It begins to hit close to home.

Close to home because I have been one of those who have mocked and made fun of others when they offered their witness to Jesus Christ. You know, the ones who are willing to stand in the public square and tell their personal story of conversion — or the church on the other side of town that worships God in a way different than mine.

Some 30 years ago, I was in the midst of my own struggle to claim Christ Jesus as my own. I had recently "felt my heart strangely warmed," to use Wesley's words, and was very active in my local church. At work, a bunch of co-workers started making fun of those who followed Christ. One turned to me and said, "Smith, this Jesus stuff just isn't that important, right?" I was trapped; what do I say? "You are right," I blurted out, and instantly felt the sting of denying my Lord. Is this what Peter felt that night he betrayed Jesus?

That bothered me a lot, for several days. I wasn't putting others to death or going into homes, dragging folks out and committing them to prison, to be sure. But I had betrayed the very promise I had recently claimed as mine.

It took a while, but in many ways this proved to be one of the most important experiences in my faith journey. Out of it came a faith much stronger, and a conscious decision to never apologize for claiming Jesus Christ as my Savior or to berate others who claimed their Savior in a way different than mine. I had denied my faith; God used that in a way that forever has changed my life. And the good news is that God can do that for you. Today.

Jerry Smith

Pray for those who carry the torch of Christ and who find themselves in some sort of prison as a result. Pray that they may find ways to keep their flame lit even in the dark times—and for their persecutors to be forgiven and transformed.

Begin with the prayer for guidance and discernment you wrote on Day 29.

Read Acts 8:4–25 slowly and prayerfully. What words or phrases stand out for you?

Now those who were scattered went from place to place, proclaiming the word. ⁵Philip went down to the city of Samaria and proclaimed the Messiah to them. ⁶The crowds with one accord listened eagerly to what was said by Philip, hearing and seeing the signs that he did, ⁷for unclean spirits, crying with loud shrieks, came out of many who were possessed; and many others who were paralyzed or lame were cured. ⁸So there was great joy in that city.

⁹Now a certain man named Simon had previously practiced magic in the city and amazed the people of Samaria, saying that he was someone great. ¹⁰All of them, from the least to the greatest, listened to him eagerly, saying, 'This man is the power of God that is called Great.' ¹¹And they listened eagerly to him because for a long time he had amazed them with his magic. ¹²But when they believed Philip, who was proclaiming the good news about the kingdom of God and the name of Jesus Christ, they were baptized, both men and women. ¹³Even Simon himself believed. After being baptized, he stayed constantly with Philip and was amazed when he saw the signs and great miracles that took place.

¹⁴Now when the apostles at Jerusalem heard that Samaria had accepted the word of God, they sent Peter and John to them. ¹⁵The two went down and prayed for them that they might receive the Holy Spirit ¹⁶(for as yet the Spirit had not come upon any of them; they had only been baptized in the name of the Lord Jesus). ¹⁷Then Peter and John laid their hands on them, and they received the Holy Spirit. ¹⁸Now when Simon saw that the Spirit was given through the laying on of the apostles' hands, he offered them money, ¹⁹saying, 'Give me also this power so that anyone on whom I lay my hands may receive the Holy Spirit.' ²⁰But Peter said to him, 'May your silver perish with you, because you thought you could obtain God's gift with money! ²¹You have no part or share in this, for your heart is not right before God. ²²Repent therefore of this wickedness of yours, and pray to the Lord that, if possible, the intent of your heart may be forgiven you. ²³For I see that you are in the gall of bitterness and the chains of wickedness.' ²⁴Simon answered, 'Pray for me to the Lord, that nothing of what you have said may happen to me.'

Reflect

What boundaries is the Gospel crossing in this text?

What boundaries has the Gospel crossed in your life? What prejudices have you overcome because of the Gospel? What prejudices are still to be overcome?

How pure are your motives when it comes to advancing the Gospel and communicating the gift of the Holy Spirit? Do you need to repent of anything?

Respond

Repent of anything you need to in order that you might be an instrument of Good News.

Encouragement: *Confrontation*

It's sad but true: We all too frequently come across people in our communities who mistakenly believe that association with "Church" is about magic or worldly power. Someone inquires about baptism clearly thinking it's a like a good luck charm for their kid, or hocus-pocus that will heal them of disease; another uses position or pocketbook as a means to throw his or her weight around, bullying others into submitting to the powerful person's opinion. It is a challenge to teach and confront with equal measures of courage and grace, as Peter did with Simon. That Peter himself had his heart "right before God" (the key) is evident in that Simon did not leave the community in a huff, but humbly asked for Peter to pray with him. May we be ready to do the same, both when we are in the position of confronting/teaching and when we are the ones confronted.

Laurie McHugh

Pray for pure motives and a clean heart so that everything you do and say fans the flame of God's mission in the world.

Begin with the prayer for guidance and discernment you wrote on Day 29.

Read Acts 8:26–40 slowly and prayerfully. What words or phrases stand out for you?

> Then an angel of the Lord said to Philip, 'Get up and go towards the south to the road that goes down from Jerusalem to Gaza.' (This is a wilderness road.) ²⁷So he got up and went. Now there was an Ethiopian eunuch, a court official of the Candace, queen of the Ethiopians, in charge of her entire treasury. He had come to Jerusalem to worship ²⁸and was returning home; seated in his chariot, he was reading the prophet Isaiah. ²⁹Then the Spirit said to Philip, 'Go over to this chariot and join it.' ³⁰So Philip ran up to it and heard him reading the prophet Isaiah. He asked, 'Do you understand what you are reading?' ³¹He replied, 'How can I, unless someone guides me?' And he invited Philip to get in and sit beside him. ³²Now the passage of the scripture that he was reading was this:
>
> > 'Like a sheep he was led to the slaughter,
> >   and like a lamb silent before its shearer,
> >   so he does not open his mouth.
> > ³³In his humiliation justice was denied him.
> >   Who can describe his generation?
> >   For his life is taken away from the earth.'
>
> ³⁴The eunuch asked Philip, 'About whom, may I ask you, does the prophet say this, about himself or about someone else?' ³⁵Then Philip began to speak, and starting with this scripture, he proclaimed to him the good news about Jesus. ³⁶As they were going along the road, they came to some water; and the eunuch said, 'Look, here is water! What is to prevent me from being baptized?' ³⁸He commanded the chariot to stop, and both of them, Philip and the eunuch, went down into the water, and Philip baptized him. ³⁹When they came up out of the water, the Spirit of the Lord snatched Philip away; the eunuch saw him no more, and went on his way rejoicing. ⁴⁰But Philip found himself at Azotus, and as he was passing through the region, he proclaimed the good news to all the towns until he came to Caesarea.

Reflect

How is the Gospel crossing another boundary?

Is there some boundary right in front of you or your church which you have not thought to cross? What would it take to cross it?

What boundaries might need a coordinated effort among churches to more effectively cross?

Respond

Cross a boundary today. Connect with someone with whom you would not normally connect.

Encouragement: *Bridges*

It doesn't take much, does it? The wrong address. A heavy accent. Too many tattoos. Unfamiliar clothing. Even missing body parts. Whatever boundary it may be, it doesn't take much to come to the conclusion — "I'm not the one."

But the Holy Spirit told Philip: "You are in the right place at the right time. You are the one for him. You are the bridge I will use to reach him." So not by his choice, but by the direction of the Spirit, Philip became the one who brought the Ethiopian eunuch face to face with God in Jesus Christ.

I have often reflected upon the fact that even today, Christian congregations in the United States are still the most segregated place in the country on Sunday morning. From what I read in the New Testament, disciples aren't deciding who becomes part of the Body of Christ, the Holy Spirit is. That is where the wild diversity comes from. Why is it, then, that most of our congregations remain significantly homogenous?

Well, I guess that's human nature. That's why we are reluctant to make disciples who are not like us. That's why we must pray to be "born again" through the Spirit that brought Philip to one searching eunuch.

Renae Extrum-Fernandez

Pray for forgiveness for the times you have judged people and created a distance between you and them. Pray for the power of the Holy Spirit to use churches and faith communities to fan the flames so that the Good News crosses all boundaries.

Begin with the prayer for guidance and discernment you wrote on Day 29.

Read 1 Peter 2:11–25 slowly and prayerfully. What words or phrases stand out for you?

¹¹Beloved, I urge you as aliens and exiles to abstain from the desires of the flesh that wage war against the soul. ¹²Conduct yourselves honorably among the Gentiles, so that, though they malign you as evildoers, they may see your honorable deeds and glorify God when he comes to judge.

¹³For the Lord's sake accept the authority of every human institution, whether of the emperor as supreme, ¹⁴or of governors, as sent by him to punish those who do wrong and to praise those who do right. ¹⁵For it is God's will that by doing right you should silence the ignorance of the foolish. ¹⁶As servants of God, live as free people, yet do not use your freedom as a pretext for evil. ¹⁷Honor everyone. Love the family of believers. Fear God. Honor the emperor.

¹⁸Slaves, accept the authority of your masters with all deference, not only those who are kind and gentle but also those who are harsh. ¹⁹For it is to your credit if, being aware of God, you endure pain while suffering unjustly. ²⁰If you endure when you are beaten for doing wrong, where is the credit in that? But if you endure when you do right and suffer for it, you have God's approval. ²¹For to this you have been called, because Christ also suffered for you, leaving you an example, so that you should follow in his steps.

> *²²'He committed no sin,*
> *and no deceit was found in his mouth.'*

²³When he was abused, he did not return abuse; when he suffered, he did not threaten; but he entrusted himself to the one who judges justly. ²⁴He himself bore our sins in his body on the cross, so that, free from sins, we might live for righteousness; by his wounds you have been healed. ²⁵For you were going astray like sheep, but now you have returned to the shepherd and guardian of your souls.

Joining a Movement of God's Mission in the World

Reflect

What struggle ("war") are you facing which Christ can help you overcome?

What is the right use of our freedom?

What is the main point of verses 18-25?

Respond

Make all your actions today honorable so that they give glory to God.

Encouragement: *Justice and Holiness*

When I was in college, we were at "war" against our own government (in the form of student demonstrations). The catch phrase was "justice." At that time the advice of 1 Peter 2:13, "Accept the authority of every human institution," bothered me. That could be easily abused by the authorities, as we had seen in slavery.

As I am getting older, I am thinking a lot about "holiness" more than about "justice." These days, not many people are seeking "holiness." Some even think that the word, "holiness," should be banned or not used. I believe, however, we have to achieve "holiness" and make a "holy nation" in our country and on earth for world peace!

Justice demands a fair share for everybody. Holiness asks sacrifice of my share for others. In a just society, everybody can have his or her own rights be protected. In a holy society, everybody would sacrifice his or her own rights to serve others better. If we are trying to make a just society and demanding justice, the whole world will be in continuous revenge as we have seen in the Middle East. If we are working together to make a holy society and asking forgiveness and sacrifices, the whole world will be in peace.

Some people do not want to use the term, "holiness," and use "restorative justice" as an alternative to the "retributive justice." Restorative Justice was experimented with in South Africa. Instead of taking revenge, Nelson Mandela took steps for reconciliation and peace-making in and for his country. He forgave his enemies and suggested working together for a new society. That was a "holy" decision. Holiness includes more than what justice can do.

When we emphasize "justice" we are focusing on legal due process and fair share. We need more lawyers and complicated law systems, which will be far from perfection. People will still figure out how to avoid legal charges and to meet their own needs without being caught. When we emphasize "holiness," however, we are focusing on accountability and sacrifices. We will have many responsible citizens and healthy relationships, which will promote growing together. In other words, we want to raise caring, loving, and sharing citizens who are more than legal, righteous, and self-sustaining.

Peace and "Justice" cannot go together. Peace will go hand in hand with "Holiness." Peace without justice is a fake peace. Peace with justice is a forced peace. Only peace with holiness is genuine peace. Let us go beyond "right" answer and "just" relationships to find "holy" answers and "caring" relationships.

Sungho Lee

Pray for your ability to, as a servant of God, accept the authority of human institutions and do right to extinguish ignorance and fan the flame of righteousness. Pray for your pastor, your mayor, your governor, and our President.

Week 6

It is all about amazing love (John); a love which commissions a persecutor and includes a Gentile (Acts). The conversion of Paul shows the power in the fire of Christ's love.

The opening of the Christian movement to the Gentiles demonstrates that this fire darts about in unexpected ways. This amazing love causes one to bless when others revile and to return good for evil (First Peter). Allow this love to seek the wellbeing of all regardless of any human categories that might seek to divide. As people in your congregation treat one another and strangers with unconditional love, your relationships will become more positive and synergistic. You will find yourself more open to new people, younger people, and possibly people who don't think, look or act like you.

Though we can't think alike,
may we not love alike?
May we not be of one heart,
though we are not of one opinion?
'Is thine heart right,
as my heart is with thy heart?'…
'if it be, give me thine hand.'

John Wesley,
18th Century Anglican priest and
founder of the Methodist renewal movement

Pray for guidance and discernment. If you wish, write that prayer here and use it for the next six days.

Read John 14:15–21 slowly and prayerfully. What words or phrases stand out for you?

> *"If you love me, you will keep my commandments. ¹⁶And I will ask the Father, and he will give you another Advocate, to be with you forever. ¹⁷This is the Spirit of truth, whom the world cannot receive, because it neither sees him nor knows him. You know him, because he abides with you, and he will be in you.*
>
> *¹⁸"I will not leave you orphaned; I am coming to you. ¹⁹In a little while the world will no longer see me, but you will see me; because I live, you also will live. ²⁰On that day you will know that I am in my Father, and you in me, and I in you. ²¹They who have my commandments and keep them are those who love me; and those who love me will be loved by my Father, and I will love them and reveal myself to them."*

Reflect

Do you love Christ? Do you keep His commandments? Or do you struggle with a competing motive?

According to this passage, what is the role of the Holy Spirit in your life?

What commandments is Jesus talking about?

Respond

Show Jesus Christ how much you love Him.

Encouragement: *'If You Love Me'*

Do I love you, Lord? In my head I know that it is all about love — loving God and loving my neighbor. In my mind, I'm convinced that love fulfills all the law and the prophets. In my intellect, I am sure that if I do not have love, I have nothing. I have been taught well.

But do I love you, Lord? What my head knows, my heart contradicts. I find myself attached to too many things. I cling to realities that are passing away. I can't seem to detach from these bondages by willpower, good theology, or moral clarity. In my head I want to love you, but honestly my heart has other desires and distractions that are more powerful than my mind. I am defeated and at the end of myself.

Today as I reach the limit of my capacity to unite my head and my heart, I receive a strange knowledge. It's clearly not coming from within me (for I've reached the end of me), but from beyond me. It is the Spirit of truth. Somehow, through no effort of my own, I see not only that Jesus is in God and God in Jesus, but that Jesus is in me! My heart clings to Christ and my head celebrates this gift. Yes, I do love you Lord, but even this is a precious gift from you.

May this gift spread wildly in a world so desperate for integrity of mind and heart.

Blake Busick

Pray for those who feel that they are alone in this world, that we might reach them with the love of Christ so that the movement of God's mission in the world spreads more wildly.

DAY 37

Begin with the prayer for guidance and discernment you wrote on Day 36.

Read Acts 9:1–22 slowly and prayerfully. What words or phrases stand out for you?

> Meanwhile Saul, still breathing threats and murder against the disciples of the Lord, went to the high priest ²and asked him for letters to the synagogues at Damascus, so that if he found any who belonged to the Way, men or women, he might bring them bound to Jerusalem. ³Now as he was going along and approaching Damascus, suddenly a light from heaven flashed around him. ⁴He fell to the ground and heard a voice saying to him, "Saul, Saul, why do you persecute me?" 5He asked, "Who are you, Lord?" The reply came, "I am Jesus, whom you are persecuting. ⁶But get up and enter the city, and you will be told what you are to do." ⁷The men who were traveling with him stood speechless because they heard the voice but saw no one. ⁸Saul got up from the ground, and though his eyes were open, he could see nothing; so they led him by the hand and brought him into Damascus. ⁹For three days he was without sight, and neither ate nor drank.
>
> ¹⁰Now there was a disciple in Damascus named Ananias. The Lord said to him in a vision, "Ananias." He answered, "Here I am, Lord." ¹¹The Lord said to him, "Get up and go to the street called Straight, and at the house of Judas look for a man of Tarsus named Saul. At this moment he is praying, ¹²and he has seen in a vision a man named Ananias come in and lay his hands on him so that he might regain his sight." ¹³But Ananias answered, "Lord, I have heard from many about this man, how much evil he has done to your saints in Jerusalem; ¹⁴and here he has authority from the chief priests to bind all who invoke your name." ¹⁵But the Lord said to him, "Go, for he is an instrument whom I have chosen to bring my name before Gentiles and kings and before the people of Israel; ¹⁶I myself will show him how much he must suffer for the sake of my name." ¹⁷So Ananias went and entered the house. He laid his hands on Saul and said, "Brother Saul, the Lord Jesus, who appeared to you on your way here, has sent me so that you may regain your sight and be filled with the Holy Spirit." ¹⁸And immediately something like scales fell from his eyes, and his sight was restored. Then he got up and was baptized, ¹⁹and after taking some food, he regained his strength. For several days he was with the disciples in Damascus, ²⁰and immediately he began to proclaim Jesus in the synagogues, saying, "He is the Son of God." ²¹All

who heard him were amazed and said, "Is not this the man who made havoc in Jerusalem among those who invoked this name? And has he not come here for the purpose of bringing them bound before the chief priests?" ²²Saul became increasingly more powerful and confounded the Jews who lived in Damascus by proving that Jesus was the Messiah.

Reflect

Have you ever had an Ananias experience? Either someone who was God-sent to help the scales fall from your eyes, or being sent by God to deliver someone?

Does God have your attention today? What has the Lord had to do to get your attention in the past?

Think of someone you personally know who seems the most resistant to Christ. Is it possible that he or she is a spiritual leader in the making? What difference might it make if you started to see and act toward that person, utilizing that perspective?

Respond

Make an appointment to have a conversation with the person you named above.

Encouragement: *Radically Open to the Leading of the Spirit*

Jesus' announcement that his followers would be his *witnesses in Jerusalem, Judea, Samaria and to the ends of the earth* (Acts 1:8) takes on a whole new dimension with the inclusion of the persecutor Saul into the Jesus movement. It has been amazing to me to reflect on this movement during these 50 days and pay attention to the many surprising twists and turns it takes. It doesn't progress according to the apostles' carefully defined strategy. They have a mission that will take them to the "ends of the earth," but how that unfolds is surprising.

I think being clear on a mission and even developing strategies to accomplish that mission is an important task. However, what I have rediscovered from the book of Acts is that I need to be very flexible with those strategies and cultivate an extreme sensitivity to the leading and prompting of the Holy Spirit who may empower those strategies or may surprise me with different ones. I also need to be radically open to the people God may use to accomplish this mission. They may be the very people I think are the least likely candidates.

Blake Busick

Pray for this person that God would get his or her attention and use you as a means to spread the Gospel wildly.

Begin with the prayer for guidance and discernment you wrote on Day 36.

Read Acts 9:23–31 slowly and prayerfully. What words or phrases stand out for you?

> After some time had passed, the Jews plotted to kill him, ²⁴but their plot became known to Saul. They were watching the gates day and night so that they might kill him; ²⁵but his disciples took him by night and let him down through an opening in the wall, lowering him in a basket. ²⁶When he had come to Jerusalem, he attempted to join the disciples; and they were all afraid of him, for they did not believe that he was a disciple. ²⁷But Barnabas took him, brought him to the apostles, and described for them how on the road he had seen the Lord, who had spoken to him, and how in Damascus he had spoken boldly in the name of Jesus. ²⁸So he went in and out among them in Jerusalem, speaking boldly in the name of the Lord. ²⁹He spoke and argued with the Hellenists; but they were attempting to kill him. ³⁰When the believers learned of it, they brought him down to Caesarea and sent him off to Tarsus. ³¹Meanwhile the church throughout Judea, Galilee, and Samaria had peace and was built up. Living in the fear of the Lord and in the comfort of the Holy Spirit, it increased in numbers.

Reflect

Are you more of a Saul/Paul or a Barnabas?

If a Barnabas, where do you need to mediate and encourage Christians who fear (or are alienated from) one another?

If a Saul/Paul, how are you using your influence and tenacity to spread the fire?

In verse 31 there is another reference to the Church increasing in numbers. How do you account for this? What is the reason for or cause of the growth? What is preventing a similar phenomenon in our churches today?

Respond

Begin living out your identified Barnabas or Saul opportunity to spread the reign of God.

Encouragement: *Unbelievable Discipleship*

The claim that Saul/Paul was a disciple was met with no shortages of scoffers and grumblers. People reacted with wonder, disbelief, and even fear. How could HE become a follower of Christ? What qualifies HIM? With so many people to choose from, why would God pick the worst of us to be a proclaimer of good news and a bearer of God's light to the world?

I have had the honor of knowing a disciple in the streets of Sanger. Troy Rogers lived his entire life in Sanger and was well known in the community; but when he died, even his mother was surprised to know that he was in regular attendance at our church. Troy struggled with alcoholism and he lived at the park. Troy had long since stopped attempting to fit into the expectations of the good people of Sanger, but that did not mean that he stopped wanting to love and be loved. Troy was known for his random acts of love — sharing what he had with others, offering himself in labor with no expectations, being a compassionate presence. Yet more often than not, Troy was feared in polite circles. Why is he here? What is that smell? Is that alcohol? Does he want money? Is he just here for the food?

What I found in Troy, like in Saul/Paul, was unbelievable discipleship. Remembering Troy's constant presence and his unwillingness to enter past the chairs in the back of the sanctuary, I am reminded of the Pharisee and the Publican. Some of us are so aware of our shortcomings that we don't feel comfortable in the liturgical life that we usually see in church. Maybe we can't lift our hands to God in a church. Maybe we can't sing all the hymns from memory. Maybe we can't even come to the Altar and pray on our knees. Yet still we come to the temple and pound our chest, quietly; almost silently we whisper, "Lord, have mercy on me." Troy's unbelievable discipleship inspires me and many others. He shows us that God's love reaches beyond our poor behavior, God's love moves us beyond our circumstances, and God allows us to live eternally and abundantly in each and every moment. Most importantly, unbelievable discipleship is about God's greatness instead of our qualifications.

Deep down inside I know that if you knew me as I do, you would think that my discipleship is unbelievable, too. The good news is that God can use unbelievable discipleship to bring peace and growth to the church.

Thanks be to God.

George Bennett

Pray for the unity and growth of the Church and her believers. Pray for the wild spread of God's reign.

Begin with the prayer for guidance and discernment you wrote on Day 36.

Read Acts 9:32–42 slowly and prayerfully. What words or phrases stand out for you?

> Now as Peter went here and there among all the believers, he came down also to the saints living in Lydda. ³³There he found a man named Aeneas, who had been bedridden for eight years, for he was paralyzed. ³⁴Peter said to him, "Aeneas, Jesus Christ heals you; get up and make your bed!" And immediately he got up. ³⁵And all the residents of Lydda and Sharon saw him and turned to the Lord.
>
> ³⁶Now in Joppa there was a disciple whose name was Tabitha, which in Greek is Dorcas. She was devoted to good works and acts of charity. ³⁷At that time she became ill and died. When they had washed her, they laid her in a room upstairs. ³⁸Since Lydda was near Joppa, the disciples, who heard that Peter was there, sent two men to him with the request, "Please come to us without delay." ³⁹So Peter got up and went with them; and when he arrived, they took him to the room upstairs. All the widows stood beside him, weeping and showing tunics and other clothing that Dorcas had made while she was with them. ⁴⁰Peter put all of them outside, and then he knelt down and prayed. He turned to the body and said, "Tabitha, get up." Then she opened her eyes, and seeing Peter, she sat up. ⁴¹He gave her his hand and helped her up. Then calling the saints and widows, he showed her to be alive. ⁴²This became known throughout Joppa, and many believed in the Lord.

Reflect

This is yet another story of healing as a means of spreading the gospel. What healing—or other sign and wonder—is happening in your community of faith which, if it were known, would draw more people to Christ?

Peter's reputation was as a healer. Tabitha's reputation was as one who was devoted to good works and acts of charity. What kind of reputation is God creating in you?

Respond

Spend time with two or three other people from your community of faith and make a plan for getting the word out about what God is up to in your ministry setting.

Encouragement: *Best Kept Secrets*

As I read today's reading the phrase "best kept secret" came to mind. It is often used when describing a destination or eating establishment, which has great offerings that not many people know about. Sound familiar? As I travel throughout the Conference and in and out of many communities, the reputations of our churches and their ministries do not match what is really happening in those faith communities.

We have such amazing things happening that if more people knew about them, they would be drawn to Christ and to be a part of these faith communities. We have outreach for the poor, the sick, the lonely, and the oppressed. We have open doors, hearts, and minds for all to have a place and be welcome. We are creative and passionate and care deeply for the communities in which we live and for the world at large. I am often in awe of the many ways we live out "God moments" to transform lives. However, the key is to get beyond being a "best kept secret" and get the word out about "what God's up to" in your ministry setting.

This made me think of the many community "tables" I sit around, and how almost never is the faith community represented and bringing to the table what "God is up to" as it relates to the purpose or work of those around the table. I often find myself saying, "Well, I know of a church that…." and more times than not, I get the response, "Really?"….

We need to "make a plan" to change our reputation of being an aging, declining faith community, and find opportunities to get the word out about what "God is up to" in our ministry settings.

Kelly Newell

Pray for a rhythm in your daily life that allows for Godly interruptions. Pray for God's continued transformation of lives and communities in ways that allows the word of God's hope, love, and grace to spread wildly.

Begin with the prayer for guidance and discernment you wrote on Day 36.

Read Acts 10:1–33 slowly and prayerfully. What words or phrases stand out for you?

In Caesarea there was a man named Cornelius, a centurion of the Italian Cohort, as it was called. ²He was a devout man who feared God with all his household; he gave alms generously to the people and prayed constantly to God. ³One afternoon at about three o"clock he had a vision in which he clearly saw an angel of God coming in and saying to him, "Cornelius." ⁴He stared at him in terror and said, "What is it, Lord?" He answered, "Your prayers and your alms have ascended as a memorial before God. ⁵Now send men to Joppa for a certain Simon who is called Peter; ⁶he is lodging with Simon, a tanner, whose house is by the seaside." ⁷When the angel who spoke to him had left, he called two of his slaves and a devout soldier from the ranks of those who served him, ⁸and after telling them everything, he sent them to Joppa.

⁹About noon the next day, as they were on their journey and approaching the city, Peter went up on the roof to pray. ¹⁰He became hungry and wanted something to eat; and while it was being prepared, he fell into a trance. ¹¹He saw the heaven opened and something like a large sheet coming down, being lowered to the ground by its four corners. ¹²In it were all kinds of four-footed creatures and reptiles and birds of the air. ¹³Then he heard a voice saying, "Get up, Peter; kill and eat." ¹⁴But Peter said, "By no means, Lord; for I have never eaten anything that is profane or unclean." ¹⁵The voice said to him again, a second time, "What God has made clean, you must not call profane." ¹⁶This happened three times, and the thing was suddenly taken up to heaven. ¹⁷Now while Peter was greatly puzzled about what to make of the vision that he had seen, suddenly the men sent by Cornelius appeared. They were asking for Simon's house and were standing by the gate. ¹⁸They called out to ask whether Simon, who was called Peter, was staying there.

¹⁹While Peter was still thinking about the vision, the Spirit said to him, "Look, three men are searching for you. ²⁰Now get up, go down, and go with them without hesitation; for I have sent them." ²¹So Peter went down to the men and said, "I am the one you are looking for; what is the reason for your coming?" ²²They answered, "Cornelius, a centurion, an upright and God-fearing man, who is well

spoken of by the whole Jewish nation, was directed by a holy angel to send for you to come to his house and to hear what you have to say." *23*So Peter invited them in and gave them lodging. The next day he got up and went with them, and some of the believers from Joppa accompanied him. *24*The following day they came to Caesarea. Cornelius was expecting them and had called together his relatives and close friends. *25*On Peter's arrival Cornelius met him, and falling at his feet, worshiped him. *26*But Peter made him get up, saying, "Stand up; I am only a mortal." *27*And as he talked with him, he went in and found that many had assembled; *28*and he said to them, "You yourselves know that it is unlawful for a Jew to associate with or to visit a Gentile; but God has shown me that I should not call anyone profane or unclean. *29*So when I was sent for, I came without objection. Now may I ask why you sent for me?" *30*Cornelius replied, "Four days ago at this very hour, at three o"clock, I was praying in my house when suddenly a man in dazzling clothes stood before me. *31*He said, 'Cornelius, your prayer has been heard and your alms have been remembered before God. *32*Send therefore to Joppa and ask for Simon, who is called Peter; he is staying in the home of Simon, a tanner, by the sea.' *33*Therefore I sent for you immediately, and you have been kind enough to come. So now all of us are here in the presence of God to listen to all that the Lord has commanded you to say."

Reflect

Once again we see the Gospel crossing another boundary. What obstacles had to be overcome before this boundary was crossed? How did this happen?

What is the significance of this story to the movement of Christ's mission in the world?

What parallels can you draw between this story and our situation and opportunities today?

Respond

Act upon a prompting of the Holy Spirit to include someone in your life or faith community whom you never saw a way to include before.

Encouragement: *The Foundations for Who We Are*

Our meditation reminds me that one of the great things about a multi-cultural family is that, regardless of our language barrier, our actions speak louder than words. We have a church family where there are African-Americans, Caucasians, Tongans, and Asians. We are a very diverse Church but at the same time the spirit of our faith, love, and respect to each others' cultures binds us together as one family. Put us together in a worship service, choir, potluck, dancing, and fellowship — and what a powerful and mighty force of love in action, in mission, and in outreach that is.

A Tongan former NFL player said, "We Tongans benefit from Dr. Martin Luther King's dream and the African-Americans' struggles through slavery and racism." I am very thankful for those who came before us and prepared a place, The United Methodist Church, where we call home. Thanks to them for their stewardship of their lives to lay the foundation where we, the latecomers, benefit.

Sifa Hingano

Pray that radical hospitality would be a part of your lifestyle and the character of your faith community so that the light of Christ might spread more wildly.

Begin with the prayer for guidance and discernment you wrote on Day 36.

Read Acts 10:34–48 slowly and prayerfully. What words or phrases stand out for you?

> *Then Peter began to speak to them: "I truly understand that God shows no partiality, ³⁵but in every nation anyone who fears him and does what is right is acceptable to him. ³⁶You know the message he sent to the people of Israel, preaching peace by Jesus Christ—he is Lord of all. ³⁷That message spread throughout Judea, beginning in Galilee after the baptism that John announced: ³⁸how God anointed Jesus of Nazareth with the Holy Spirit and with power; how he went about doing good and healing all who were oppressed by the devil, for God was with him. ³⁹We are witnesses to all that he did both in Judea and in Jerusalem. They put him to death by hanging him on a tree; ⁴⁰but God raised him on the third day and allowed him to appear, ⁴¹not to all the people but to us who were chosen by God as witnesses, and who ate and drank with him after he rose from the dead. ⁴²He commanded us to preach to the people and to testify that he is the one ordained by God as judge of the living and the dead. ⁴³All the prophets testify about him that everyone who believes in him receives forgiveness of sins through his name."*
>
> *⁴⁴While Peter was still speaking, the Holy Spirit fell upon all who heard the word. ⁴⁵The circumcised believers who had come with Peter were astounded that the gift of the Holy Spirit had been poured out even on the Gentiles, ⁴⁶for they heard them speaking in tongues and extolling God. Then Peter said, ⁴⁷"Can anyone withhold the water for baptizing these people who have received the Holy Spirit just as we have?" ⁴⁸So he ordered them to be baptized in the name of Jesus Christ. Then they invited him to stay for several days.*

Reflect

In your heart do you know and believe that God shows no partiality?

What needs to change in your life and church to make the Gospel more accessible to those who would assume that Christ (or your faith community) was "not for them"?

How has the Holy Spirit surprised you recently?

Respond

Think of how welcoming your faith community is, from the point of view of someone who has no church background. Implement one idea to make it more accessible to them.

Encouragement: *Spirit*

The scripture tells me that the Spirit blows where it will.

If that is true, then we do not command, call, beckon or create the Spirit.

"While Peter was still speaking…" It may have been like the baby who cries just before your brilliant closing sentence. Distraction? Emphasis? The real point?

What is my role? I'm a witness.

I report what I see. "You again!" as the writer Annie Dillard phrases it.

It is not my job to screen the audience. It is my job to tell the truth as best I can. To report the awe and wonder. To nod toward the mystery. To weep at the beauty.

It is my job to hear the witness of others, as well. Who knows — while they are still speaking, the Spirit might just drop by and stay awhile.

Ted Virts

Pray that your faith community and all faith communities will not only welcome the "Corneliuses" of the world, but will go to where they live in order to do so.

Begin with the prayer for guidance and discernment you wrote on Day 36.

Read 1 Peter 3 slowly and prayerfully. What words or phrases stand out for you?

Wives, in the same way, accept the authority of your husbands, so that, even if some of them do not obey the word, they may be won over without a word by their wives' conduct, ²when they see the purity and reverence of your lives. ³Do not adorn yourselves outwardly by braiding your hair, and by wearing gold ornaments or fine clothing; ⁴rather, let your adornment be the inner self with the lasting beauty of a gentle and quiet spirit, which is very precious in God's sight. ⁵It was in this way long ago that the holy women who hoped in God used to adorn themselves by accepting the authority of their husbands. ⁶Thus Sarah obeyed Abraham and called him lord. You have become her daughters as long as you do what is good and never let fears alarm you. ⁷Husbands, in the same way, show consideration for your wives in your life together, paying honor to the woman as the weaker sex, since they too are also heirs of the gracious gift of life—so that nothing may hinder your prayers.

⁸Finally, all of you, have unity of spirit, sympathy, love for one another, a tender heart, and a humble mind. ⁹Do not repay evil for evil or abuse for abuse; but, on the contrary, repay with a blessing. It is for this that you were called—that you might inherit a blessing. ¹⁰For "Those who desire life and desire to see good days, let them keep their tongues from evil and their lips from speaking deceit; ¹¹let them turn away from evil and do good; let them seek peace and pursue it. ¹²For the eyes of the Lord are on the righteous, and his ears are open to their prayer. But the face of the Lord is against those who do evil." ¹³Now who will harm you if you are eager to do what is good? ¹⁴But even if you do suffer for doing what is right, you are blessed. Do not fear what they fear, and do not be intimidated, ¹⁵but in your hearts sanctify Christ as Lord. Always be ready to make your defense to anyone who demands from you an accounting for the hope that is in you;

¹⁶yet do it with gentleness and reverence. Keep your conscience clear, so that, when you are maligned, those who abuse you for your good conduct in Christ may be put to shame. ¹⁷For it is better to suffer for doing good, if suffering should be God's will, than to suffer for doing evil.

¹⁸For Christ also suffered for sins once for all, the righteous for the unrighteous, in order to bring you to God. He was put to death in the flesh, but made alive in the spirit, ¹⁹in which also he went and made a proclamation to the spirits in prison, ²⁰who in former times did not obey, when God waited patiently in the days of Noah, during the building of the ark, in which a few, that is, eight persons, were saved through water.

²¹And baptism, which this prefigured, now saves you—not as a removal of dirt from the body, but as an appeal to God for a good conscience, through the resurrection of Jesus Christ, ²²who has gone into heaven and is at the right hand of God, with angels, authorities, and powers made subject to him.

Reflect

How would you apply the example of Christ's suffering to your life today? Where does it have practical application?

When was the last time you repaid evil with a blessing? Are you prepared to do so in the future?

How would you describe the hope which is within you?

Respond

Do some good today. Repay an evil with good.

Encouragement: *Being a Part of the Movement*

Certainly, this "Catch Fire in 50 Days" study encourages us toward being a part of the huge cosmic/eternal "movement of grace transforming the world."

However, often the "huge-ness" of this mission seems, well … just so/ too huge!

Ah, but just in good time, the scripture calls out: "Finally, all of you, have unity of spirit, sympathy, love for one another, a tender heart, and a humble mind …. Let [those who desire life and desire to see good days] turn away from evil and do good; let them seek peace and pursue it …. in your hearts sanctify Christ as Lord. Always be ready to make your defense to anyone who demands from you an accounting for the hope that is in you." (1 Peter 3).

With this scripture, the huge-ness of our mission becomes more individualized and accessible. It seems to become "way" less dramatic. But is this, also, way less effective?

Have you seen those ads on television where one person's good — often life-saving — act, becomes a chain reaction of goodness?

It seems to happen as one person, a carrier of goodness, lives out an action of goodness. When "others" see that action, they are impressed. One can almost hear the "others" say, "Wow!" or "That's so great!" or even just give approving sighs. The "others" — and perhaps we, too — are infected. We are exposed to the virus of goodness.

The "others," (perhaps we) become a part of the chain reaction of goodness that continues. The goodness, as they say, "goes viral."

Imagine the fire of the Holy Spirit, the message of the Gospel, "going viral" every time any one of us might testify to the hope that is within us. Such individual word or action would be huge. Such would certainly be in the realm of what is cosmic and eternal! And, such would be, and is, in the realm of what we can and are called to do.

When I see that television ad, I generally start humming the hymn-song that sings out:

"It only takes a spark to get a fire going.

And soon all those around, will warm up to its glowing.

That's how it is with God's love, once you experience it.

You spread his love to everyone. You want to pass it on."

We certainly can — and must — be amidst this "movement of grace transforming the world."

Mariellen Yoshino

Pray for all who will be gathering for worship tomorrow that they would expect and encounter the Living Christ in a way which sets them on fire to join the movement of God's mission for the world.

Week 7

Jesus prays for the unity of those who have received him. Unity gives credibility to the movement that is our message and mission (John).

As the fire of the movement spreads (even unexpectedly), the Church has to adapt its theology and practice to incorporate the new work of the Holy Spirit.

Thus, Peter must explain to the Church in Jerusalem how it was that the Gospel was given to the Gentiles. Pressure from without continues. Meanwhile, from within, missionaries are commissioned (Acts). The Way of Jesus is not easy, but we are reassured of God's support, strength and grace (First Peter).

What new fire is God calling your congregation to start?

What is your role in that personally?

There is a grandeur in the uniformity of the mass. When a fashion, a dance, a song, a slogan or a joke sweeps like wildfire from one end of the continent to the other, and a hundred million people roar with laughter, sway their bodies in unison, hum one song or break forth in anger and denunciation, there is the overpowering feeling that in this country we have come nearer the brotherhood of man than ever before.

Eric Hoffer,
American Writer (1902-1983)

When you are kind to someone in trouble, you hope they'll remember and be kind to someone else. And it'll become like a wildfire.

Whoopi Goldberg,
American Actress, Comedian and Singer. b.1955)

Pray for guidance and discernment. If you wish, write that prayer here and use it for the next six days.

Read John 17:1–11 slowly and prayerfully. What words or phrases stand out for you?

> After Jesus had spoken these words, he looked up to heaven and said, "Father, the hour has come; glorify your Son so that the Son may glorify you, ²since you have given him authority over all people, to give eternal life to all whom you have given him. ³And this is eternal life, that they may know you, the only true God, and Jesus Christ whom you have sent. ⁴I glorified you on earth by finishing the work that you gave me to do. ⁵So now, Father, glorify me in your own presence with the glory that I had in your presence before the world existed.
>
> ⁶"I have made your name known to those whom you gave me from the world. They were yours, and you gave them to me, and they have kept your word. ⁷Now they know that everything you have given me is from you; ⁸for the words that you gave to me I have given to them, and they have received them and know in truth that I came from you; and they have believed that you sent me. ⁹I am asking on their behalf; I am not asking on behalf of the world, but on behalf of those whom you gave me, because they are yours. ¹⁰All mine are yours, and yours are mine; and I have been glorified in them.
>
> ¹¹And now I am no longer in the world, but they are in the world, and I am coming to you. Holy Father, protect them in your name that you have given me, so that they may be one, as we are one.

Reflect

What is the "hour" to which Jesus refers? How will He be glorified in this? How will this enable you to know the only true God?

Why is the unity of Jesus' followers so important? What is the source of that unity? What are its characteristics?

What is the relationship between unity and evangelism?

Respond

Share your ideas for how to create and show unity among one or more of the following:
- our churches and faith communities;
- faith communities of other traditions and denominations.

You may share this on the Facebook page (**www.facebook.com/catchfirein50**) or directly with your pastor or other faith leader.

Encouragement: *Oneness*

"Holy Father, protect them … so that they may be one, as we are one."

The famous South Indian evangelist D.T. Niles once preached, "Evangelism is one hungry man telling another where to find the bread." As much as our differences divide us, Christians have something very powerful that unites us, which we tend to forget.

The notion of a perfect unity in the body of Christ at its origins is an idealistic myth. After all, why did Paul write all those epistles, other than to encourage the young Christians to get along?!

Today there is no denying that we are separated by doctrine, politics, race and gender, age, social status, and sexual orientation. Fueled by suspicion and competition as we are, our differences drive us to prejudice and isolation. Our differences splinter the light of Christ into the denominational prism.

As he prepares his disciples for his arrest and crucifixion, Jesus reminds them in the gospel of John that he and God are one, just as Jesus has been one with them. He prays that God would protect their unity in Christ that they might be one with God.

When the differences between us are stripped away, when pride, heritage and status are put aside, aren't we all lost and wounded children yearning to be found? Isn't our desperate longing to make sense of this life and find a home in it something we all share?

All-too-often it takes failure or tragedy for us sophisticated, self-sufficient North Americans to get to that point — to really feel our hunger to love and be loved by something greater than ourselves. The Church that offers such bread will thrive in the future; it always has. The church that invests in its differences will eventually wither away.

Gracious God, bind us together Lord, bind us together with hearts that cannot be broken … In Jesus' Name. Amen.

Mark Bollwinkel

Pray for the unity of the Church and our credibility in the world so that we might start more Holy Spirit fires without extinguishing each other's fire.

Begin with the prayer for guidance and discernment you wrote on Day 43.

Read Acts 11:1–18 slowly and prayerfully. What words or phrases stand out for you?

> *Now the apostles and the believers who were in Judea heard that the Gentiles had also accepted the word of God. ²So when Peter went up to Jerusalem, the circumcised believers criticized him, ³saying, "Why did you go to uncircumcised men and eat with them?" ⁴Then Peter began to explain it to them, step by step, saying, ⁵"I was in the city of Joppa praying, and in a trance I saw a vision. There was something like a large sheet coming down from heaven, being lowered by its four corners; and it came close to me. ⁶As I looked at it closely I saw four-footed animals, beasts of prey, reptiles, and birds of the air. ⁷I also heard a voice saying to me, 'Get up, Peter; kill and eat.' ⁸But I replied, 'By no means, Lord; for nothing profane or unclean has ever entered my mouth.' ⁹But a second time the voice answered from heaven, 'What God has made clean, you must not call profane.' ¹⁰This happened three times; then everything was pulled up again to heaven. ¹¹At that very moment three men, sent to me from Caesarea, arrived at the house where we were. ¹²The Spirit told me to go with them and not to make a distinction between them and us. These six brothers also accompanied me, and we entered the man's house. ¹³He told us how he had seen the angel standing in his house and saying, 'Send to Joppa and bring Simon, who is called Peter; ¹⁴he will give you a message by which you and your entire household will be saved.' ¹⁵And as I began to speak, the Holy Spirit fell upon them just as it had upon us at the beginning. ¹⁶And I remembered the word of the Lord, how he had said, 'John baptized with water, but you will be baptized with the Holy Spirit.' ¹⁷If then God gave them the same gift that he gave us when we believed in the Lord Jesus Christ, who was I that I could hinder God?" ¹⁸When they heard this, they were silenced. And they praised God, saying, "Then God has given even to the Gentiles the repentance that leads to life."*

Reflect

Consider how extraordinary an event was the inclusion of the Gentiles in the Church. How did it happen? Are there parallels in your context?

How might you be a more effective witness to the new things the Holy Spirit might be doing in your midst?

Throughout this study we have been reading about the Gospel spreading like wildfire. Yet all this happened without a strategic plan. It often happened unexpectedly, even when there was intense opposition from without and tension from within. How do you explain this? What can you apply from this reflection to your current context?

Respond

Identify a place or a people in which God might be calling you to start a fire.

Encouragement: *Silences*

Today I am totally focused on verse 18. I am thinking about what was happening during the silence. Peter delivered his message, which God gave them — the same gift that he gave us when we believed in the Lord Jesus Christ. And then there was silence.

What was going on in the minds and hearts of the crowd listening to Peter? Did they become concerned that they were no longer in control? Did they begin to think of ways to teach these new folks how to act, now that they are a part of us? Were there some who had feelings of resentment because new people, different people, might not appreciate all the hard work and sacrifice that had been made thus far?

We don't know how long the silence lasted on that day. Something pretty powerful must have been going on. People were being told that the movement was taking a different turn. That new and different people would be included in this new reign of God. The reaction out of the silence was not that of fear, but of praise. The people praised God with a new appreciation for the power of God's Holy Spirit to bring salvation to all.

I pray that out of the silent moments of reflection from our shared study we, too, would respond with praise for all that is being made new.

Linda Caldwell

Pray for congregations and gatherings of Christians everywhere, that all will be filled with the Holy Spirit, "catch fire" and contribute to the movement of God's mission in the world.

Begin with the prayer for guidance and discernment you wrote on Day 43.

Read Acts 11:19–30 slowly and prayerfully. What words or phrases stand out for you?

> Now those who were scattered because of the persecution that took place over Stephen traveled as far as Phoenicia, Cyprus, and Antioch, and they spoke the word to no one except Jews. [20]But among them were some men of Cyprus and Cyrene who, on coming to Antioch, spoke to the Hellenists also, proclaiming the Lord Jesus. [21]The hand of the Lord was with them, and a great number became believers and turned to the Lord. [22]News of this came to the ears of the church in Jerusalem, and they sent Barnabas to Antioch. [23]When he came and saw the grace of God, he rejoiced, and he exhorted them all to remain faithful to the Lord with steadfast devotion; [24]for he was a good man, full of the Holy Spirit and of faith. And a great many people were brought to the Lord. [25]Then Barnabas went to Tarsus to look for Saul, [26]and when he had found him, he brought him to Antioch. So it was that for an entire year they met with the church and taught a great many people, and it was in Antioch that the disciples were first called "Christians."
>
> [27]At that time prophets came down from Jerusalem to Antioch. [28]One of them named Agabus stood up and predicted by the Spirit that there would be a severe famine over all the world; and this took place during the reign of Claudius. [29]The disciples determined that according to their ability, each would send relief to the believers living in Judea; [30]this they did, sending it to the elders by Barnabas and Saul.

Reflect

What made the church in Antioch so vital?

What was their connection to the church in Jerusalem?

Identify the various roles acted out by each person in this text (e.g., Barnabas, Agabus, disciples, Saul). Looking at your church, are these various roles being played?

Respond

Consider how you might help meet a need of another faith community (other than your own) in your town. Share that with your pastor.

Encouragement: *Making a Name*

Do you really think "they will know we are Christians by our love, by our love?" What if they do? Will that mean we are accepted, appreciated, or even welcome?

There are no guarantees. In a hostile environment, facing persecution, aware of the brutality one could suffer as a witness, many of Christ followers fled in fear. They chose to speak only in hushed tones, only to the familiar, only to people who would not pose a threat. Don't be a witness; you saw what happened to Stephen.

But the Spirit of boldness took hold of a few of them. They were able to proclaim Christ. To new people in unfamiliar places, the word Christ was spoken again and again. When people who have nothing are generous, when people who are scared stand, when people who are victimized can claim personhood, when people who are ashamed lift their heads, when people who persecute drop their swords, when people who are brutal embrace their victims — we ask why.

The fellowship in Antioch answered, "Christ." When our hopes are in Christ and our value comes from Christ, when our prayers are to Christ and our joy is in Christ. We pay attention to Christ in our lives, we give Christ credit, and we seek Christ's deliverance. Is it any wonder people called them Christians?

Boldness is rare in every generation. People don't want advice; we can get that anywhere. People want to know why you are so amazing. We want to know YOUR secret. How did you make it through that tragedy in your life? How did you have the strength to raise those children on your own? How did you keep hope alive in the face of death? How did you forgive the person that victimized you so brutally? How is that you have the nerve to be so happy?

Can we give credit where credit is due? Are we afraid of what they will call us? The story of the church is your story. Should it be a secret?

Be Bold.

George Bennett

Pray for God to show you who might have a prophetic word for your congregation; a word that would rekindle or fan the flames so that your faith community would become a stronger witness and further the mission of God in the world.

Begin with the prayer for guidance and discernment you wrote on Day 43.

Read Acts 12:1–19 slowly and prayerfully. What words or phrases stand out for you?

> ⁵While Peter was kept in prison, the church prayed fervently to God for him. ⁶The very night before Herod was going to bring him out, Peter, bound with two chains, was sleeping between two soldiers, while guards in front of the door were keeping watch over the prison. ⁷Suddenly an angel of the Lord appeared and a light shone in the cell. He tapped Peter on the side and woke him, saying, "Get up quickly." And the chains fell off his wrists. ⁸The angel said to him, "Fasten your belt and put on your sandals." He did so. Then he said to him, "Wrap your cloak around you and follow me." ⁹Peter went out and followed him; he did not realize that what was happening with the angel's help was real; he thought he was seeing a vision. ¹⁰After they had passed the first and the second guard, they came before the iron gate leading into the city. It opened for them of its own accord, and they went outside and walked along a lane, when suddenly the angel left him. ¹¹Then Peter came to himself and said, "Now I am sure that the Lord has sent his angel and rescued me from the hands of Herod and from all that the Jewish people were expecting." ¹²As soon as he realized this, he went to the house of Mary, the mother of John whose other name was Mark, where many had gathered and were praying. ¹³When he knocked at the outer gate, a maid named Rhoda came to answer. ¹⁴On recognizing Peter's voice, she was so overjoyed that, instead of opening the gate, she ran in and announced that Peter was standing at the gate. ¹⁵They said to her, "You are out of your mind!" But she insisted that it was so. They said, "It is his angel." ¹⁶Meanwhile Peter continued knocking; and when they opened the gate, they saw him and were amazed. ¹⁷He motioned to them with his hand to be silent, and described for them how the Lord had brought him out of the prison. And he added, "Tell this to James and to the believers." Then he left and went to another place. ¹⁸When morning came, there was no small commotion among the soldiers over what had become of Peter. ¹⁹When Herod had searched for him and could not find him, he examined the guards and ordered them to be put to death. Then Peter went down from Judea to Caesarea and stayed there.

Reflect

Do you too easily give in to worldly forces, assuming that the mission of Christ through our Church is limited because of the times in which we live? While we experience these forces often passively, the early Church experienced them actively. Does this cause you to reassess our potential as a movement of Christ's mission?

Notice the role of prayer in this story. What is the state of prayer in your life and church?

This movement in Scripture is unstoppable. What has stopped it in our context?

Respond

Gather with a few others and pray fervently to God for our deliverance from stagnation.

Encouragement: *The Distractions of Our Time*

As a person who works in young people's ministry, I think I had a different take on the reflection question that asked, "Do you too easily give in to worldly forces, assuming that the mission of Christ is limited because of the times in which we live?" What came to mind immediately was technology. Young people (OK, maybe not just the young) are robbed of their ability to make time, to take time for prayer, fellowship, and their relationship with Christ because of all the distractions that the wonderful world of technology has to offer.

When we are at camp, we ask that the staff and the campers give up their cell phones, not accepting their need to use them as a "clock, or alarm." I often am handing out drugstore watches where they actually have to read the hands of the clock! This is a shock for many to be completely "disconnected" from the "times" we live in, and experience Christ as the early church did: "actively" focused in His creation and their relationship with Him through prayer, study, fellowship, and worship. By day two there are few complaints about being without those distractions, and we have a full faith community living, praying, and seeking their potential in their life of faith. A movement of transformation happens each and every year at camp and I believe that being in His creation and participating actively in our relationship with Christ without the distractions of our times is the key.

Let us not become "stagnant" in actively experiencing and living God's mission in our lives and in the world. Remember, the focused fervent prayers of the church rescued Peter from his captors.

Kelly Newell

Pray for your pastor, that he or she might lead boldly and courageously so that others join in the movement of God's mission in the world; to once again catch on fire and spread that fire wildly.

Begin with the prayer for guidance and discernment you wrote on Day 43.

Read Acts 12:20–25 slowly and prayerfully. What words or phrases stand out for you?

> *Now Herod was angry with the people of Tyre and Sidon. So they came to him in a body; and after winning over Blastus, the king's chamberlain, they asked for a reconciliation, because their country depended on the king's country for food. ²¹On an appointed day Herod put on his royal robes, took his seat on the platform, and delivered a public address to them. ²²The people kept shouting, "The voice of a god, and not of a mortal!" ²³And immediately, because he had not given the glory to God, an angel of the Lord struck him down, and he was eaten by worms and died. ²⁴But the word of God continued to advance and gain adherents. ²⁵Then after completing their mission Barnabas and Saul returned to Jerusalem and brought with them John, whose other name was Mark.*

Reflect

> King Herod and the word of God ultimately had opposite outcomes. How do you understand power?

> In verse 24 we have another reference to growth. Why does growth seem so important?

> Is there one who you would consider to be your mission companion (a Paul to your Barnabas or a Barnabas to your Paul, etc)? If not, describe your ideal mission companion—the one who would complement your strengths.

Respond

If you have a ministry companion, call him or her today and determine what you will do together to advance the mission of God today.

If you do **not** have a ministry companion, ask God to reveal whom God has in mind.

Encouragement: *Our Calling*

This story of Herod's death and the perhaps more disturbing ones of Ananias and Sapphira — since it's a tale about believers with misguided motives who are struck down (from Acts 5:1-11, Day 23) — make it clear that God is serious about this stuff. Power, wealth, responsibility, and education — the blessings of God are not fire to be toyed with or kept to ourselves and for our security or aggrandizement, but fire that is properly used for the glory of God. It confuses us that not every person who misuses power suffers a public fall — it's quite often the opposite — and we rightly hesitate to pin causality on others' misfortunes. Still, we are called to faithfulness and fruitfulness, to look upon the world with the eyes of faith, and to partner with others to shine God's kingdom light where there is injustice and pain. We can humbly and confidently leave the ultimate results up to God.

Laurie McHugh

Pray that the churches and faith communities in your town might find community partners with whom they might start and spread more Holy Spirit fires.

Begin with the prayer for guidance and discernment you wrote on Day 43.

Read Acts 13:1–3 slowly and prayerfully. What words or phrases stand out for you?

> Now in the church at Antioch there were prophets and teachers: Barnabas, Simeon who was called Niger, Lucius of Cyrene, Manaen a member of the court of Herod the ruler, and Saul. ²While they were worshiping the Lord and fasting, the Holy Spirit said, "Set apart for me Barnabas and Saul for the work to which I have called them." ³Then after fasting and praying they laid their hands on them and sent them off.

Reflect

What is the work to which you have been called?

What is the benefit of adding fasting to praying?

Barnabas and Saul are sent off. Do you and your congregation think of yourselves as having been sent into the world?

Respond

Set a reminder alarm to go off each hour. When the alarm rings, remind yourself that you have been sent by Christ into the particular situation in which you find yourself.

Encouragement: *The Priesthood of All Believers*

This coming Sunday our congregation will participate in the baptism of my friend's son. The baby's grandfather, though now deceased, was the head usher at our church and a true disciple. He grew up a Christian in India and was one of the few folks in our congregation whom I knew had been persecuted for his faith.

As this baby is baptized, he will be incorporated by the Holy Spirit into God's new creation and made to share in Christ's royal priesthood. Our congregation will welcome him with Christian love and renew our covenant to faithfully participate in the ministries of the church by our prayers, our presence, our gifts, our service, and our witness. We will make our promises to nurture him in Christ's Holy faith and teach him to practice the Wesleyan means of grace: Prayer, Searching the Scriptures, Holy Communion, Fasting, Christian Community, and Healthy Living.

May we prepare to be sent, as this grandfather was, to share our faith. As we baptize and confirm members into our congregations and move beyond our buildings into mission and ministry in our local communities, let us remember to follow our spiritual disciplines as the church in Antioch did: They fasted and prayed and laid their hands on Barnabas and Saul and then sent them off.

Praise God for the Priesthood of all Believers, which calls each of us to minister to our faith.

Gayle Shearman

Pray for the members of churches that they will experience and be responsive to a fresh outpouring of the Holy Spirit and a wildfire spread of God's reign.

Catch Fire in 50 Days

Begin with the prayer for guidance and discernment you wrote on Day 43.

Read 1 Peter 4–5 slowly and prayerfully. What words or phrases stand out for you?

> **4** *Since therefore Christ suffered in the flesh, arm yourselves also with the same intention (for whoever has suffered in the flesh has finished with sin),* ²*so as to live for the rest of your earthly life no longer by human desires but by the will of God.* ³*You have already spent enough time in doing what the Gentiles like to do, living in licentiousness, passions, drunkenness, revels, carousing, and lawless idolatry.*
>
> ⁴*They are surprised that you no longer join them in the same excesses of dissipation, and so they blaspheme.* ⁵*But they will have to give an accounting to him who stands ready to judge the living and the dead.* ⁶*For this is the reason the gospel was proclaimed even to the dead, so that, though they had been judged in the flesh as everyone is judged, they might live in the spirit as God does.*
>
> ⁷*The end of all things is near; therefore be serious and discipline yourselves for the sake of your prayers.* ⁸*Above all, maintain constant love for one another, for love covers a multitude of sins.* ⁹*Be hospitable to one another without complaining.* ¹⁰*Like good stewards of the manifold grace of God, serve one another with whatever gift each of you has received.* ¹¹*Whoever speaks must do so as one speaking the very words of God; whoever serves must do so with the strength that God supplies, so that God may be glorified in all things through Jesus Christ. To him belong the glory and the power forever and ever. Amen.*
>
> ¹²*Beloved, do not be surprised at the fiery ordeal that is taking place among you to test you, as though something strange were happening to you.* ¹³*But rejoice insofar as you are sharing Christ's sufferings, so that you may also be glad and shout for joy when his glory is revealed.* ¹⁴*If you are reviled for the name of Christ, you are blessed, because the spirit of glory, which is the Spirit of God, is resting on you.* ¹⁵*But let none of you suffer as a murderer, a thief, a criminal, or even as a mischief maker.* ¹⁶*Yet if any of you suffers as a Christian, do not consider it a disgrace, but glorify God because you bear this name.* ¹⁷*For the time has come for judgment to begin with the household of God; if it begins with us, what will be the end for those who do not obey the gospel of God?* ¹⁸*And "If it is hard for*

the righteous to be saved, what will become of the ungodly and the sinners?" [19]Therefore, let those suffering in accordance with God's will entrust themselves to a faithful Creator, while continuing to do good.

5 Now as an elder myself and a witness of the sufferings of Christ, as well as one who shares in the glory to be revealed, I exhort the elders among you [2]to tend the flock of God that is in your charge, exercising the oversight, not under compulsion but willingly, as God would have you do it—not for sordid gain but eagerly. [3]Do not lord it over those in your charge, but be examples to the flock. [4]And when the chief shepherd appears, you will win the crown of glory that never fades away.

[5]In the same way, you who are younger must accept the authority of the elders. And all of you must clothe yourselves with humility in your dealings with one another, for "God opposes the proud, but gives grace to the humble." [6]Humble yourselves therefore under the mighty hand of God, so that he may exalt you in due time. [7]Cast all your anxiety on him, because he cares for you.

[8]Discipline yourselves, keep alert. Like a roaring lion your adversary the devil prowls around, looking for someone to devour. [9]Resist him, steadfast in your faith, for you know that your brothers and sisters in all the world are undergoing the same kinds of suffering.

[10]And after you have suffered for a little while, the God of all grace, who has called you to his eternal glory in Christ, will himself restore, support, strengthen, and establish you. [11]To him be the power forever and ever. Amen. [12]Through Silvanus, whom I consider a faithful brother, I have written this short letter to encourage you and to testify that this is the true grace of God. Stand fast in it. [13]Your sister church in Babylon, chosen together with you, sends you greetings; and so does my son Mark. [14]Greet one another with a kiss of love. Peace to all of you who are in Christ.

Reflect

What gift have you received? Are you using it in service to Christ for the glory of God?

If you are in a position of spiritual leadership, are you exercising that role willingly and not under compulsion; eagerly and not for gain?

What are you going to take with you from 1 Peter to encourage you in the difficult times—times when you feel your flame start to flicker?

Respond

Cast all anxieties on the Lord. Notice the resulting peace, humility and energy

Encouragement: *Be Examples to the Flock*

1 Peter 4 and 5 are full of practical advice, but I would sum it up in one sentence: "Do not lord it over those in your charge, but be examples to the flock." It is easy for us pastors to preach and teach, but hard to be examples.

The Bible says, "Live for the rest of your earthly life no longer by human desires but by the will of God" (1 Peter 4:2). It can mean avoiding sins of flesh (1 Peter 4:3-7). It also can mean, however, "loving one another constantly" (1 Peter 4:8-11). Both ways of being examples include enduring sufferings with complete trust in God's faithfulness while continuing to do good (1 Peter 4:12-19).

The fruits would be humility (1 Peter 5:6) and freedom from anxiety (1 Peter 5:7).

Humble yourself, then people will despise you! Humble yourself anyway.

Love enemies, then they will destroy you! Love them anyway.

If we can do this with complete trust in God's faithfulness, we can keep our fire burning and spread the sparks everywhere we go!

Sungho Lee

Pray for spiritual leaders who are exhausted and for new spiritual leaders (lay and clergy) who are called to help start more fires.

Day 50

Day 50 and Beyond: Be, See, Do

We have reached day 50, the conclusion of our study.

How will this day be different from every other day?

How will this season in our church be different from any other season?

As was stated earlier, we are approaching the dawn of a new day in our church and among our people. It is a day that will not be birthed by our plans and strategies and efforts, but by the gracious work of the Holy Spirit.

Our work is a loving response to what God is doing in our midst.

These 50 days have been an opportunity for us to pray and prepare for that new day when we as a church become a movement again.

Is that new day upon us now?

I never could stand losing.
Second place didn't interest me.
I had a fire in my belly.

Ty Cobb,
American pioneer baseball player

Life is a promise; fulfill it.

Mother Theresa,
20th century Albanian nun,
founder of The Missionaries of Charity movement

Best of all, God is with us

John Wesley

Pray for guidance and discernment.

Read John 7:37–39; Acts 2:1–13 slowly and prayerfully. What words or phrases stand out for you?

John 7:37-39

On the last day of the festival, the great day, while Jesus was standing there, he cried out, "Let anyone who is thirsty come to me, ³⁸and let the one who believes in me drink. As the scripture has said, 'Out of the believer's heart shall flow rivers of living water.'" ³⁹Now he said this about the Spirit, which believers in him were to receive; for as yet there was no Spirit, because Jesus was not yet glorified.

Acts 2:1-13

When the day of Pentecost had come, they were all together in one place. ²And suddenly from heaven there came a sound like the rush of a violent wind, and it filled the entire house where they were sitting. ³Divided tongues, as of fire, appeared among them, and a tongue rested on each of them. ⁴All of them were filled with the Holy Spirit and began to speak in other languages, as the Spirit gave them ability.

⁵Now there were devout Jews from every nation under heaven living in Jerusalem. ⁶And at this sound the crowd gathered and was bewildered, because each one heard them speaking in the native language of each. ⁷Amazed and astonished, they asked, "Are not all these who are speaking Galileans? ⁸And how is it that we hear, each of us, in our own native language? ⁹Parthians, Medes, Elamites, and residents of Mesopotamia, Judea and Cappadocia, Pontus and Asia, ¹⁰Phrygia and Pamphylia, Egypt and the parts of Libya belonging to Cyrene, and visitors from Rome, both Jews and proselytes, ¹¹Cretans and Arabs—in our own languages we hear them speaking about God's deeds of power." ¹²All were amazed and perplexed, saying to one another, "What does this mean?" ¹³But others sneered and said, "They are filled with new wine."

Reflect

In light of the last 50 days and these Pentecost texts, answer these questions as you are able for yourself, your congregation and the community of Believers:

BE who you are. Don't try to be someone you are not—individually or as a congregation. This is about fully embracing your core identity, your DNA, the way you are wired. No two people and no two congregations are the same. Gifts differ, theology differs, and passion differs. God is inviting you into ministry—this is not about the invitation to the people down the street. Write down unique, positive qualities that define your church; things about your church and its people that distinguish you from just any church.

SEE what you have. Often we focus on what we don't have. Instead you are invited to clearly see the abundance of assets in your congregation and the community. Through the *Readiness 360* inventory, churches better understand what strengths they currently bring to the table. Through intentional study of the community (both through demographic studies like *Mission Insite* and through face-to-face conversations with neighbors), churches can discern more clearly where their lives can productively intersect with the lives of their neighbors. Unless we are intentional in our looking and our listening, both within the church and within the community, we will not see what we need to see. Many churches see only their own tired assumptions or perhaps see a reality that is twenty years obsolete. Write down your assets—ministries with positive momentum, community partnerships, opportunities, talents/passions of committed participants and anything else that could be used to do great things.

DO what matters to God. Given who you are and what you have including the ministry field that God has placed around you, the question is this: ***What does God want your church to do?*** Answering this question moves us from study to action. Over the last fifty days, you have read and pondered numerous key scriptures from the New Testament. You are using the promptings and stirrings of the Holy Spirit during the 50 days along with the above assessment of your congregation and community to gain clarity of an emerging vision. Where do you sense God calling out to you and/or inviting your church into action? Share what you are sensing with others to compare notes. It is possible that many persons in your church are all sensing something very similar. What is the body sensing? Where is consensus emerging? What actions can you take now, even as you continue to pray about other things?

Respond

Identify next steps given your reflections.

Encouragement: *A Prayer for Our Future*

By your grace, O Lord, I have had a fresh encounter with you during these 50 days. I have been raised with Christ and "given a new birth into a living hope through the resurrection of Jesus Christ from the dead."

I pray that the power of your resurrection might be set loose in the world through our churches once again by the fire of the Holy Spirit. Keep rekindling this gift that is within us, that we might join the movement that is your mission in the world. We need your presence to keep the fire burning, that your light might shine brightly through us. We depend upon your love to keep fanning the flame and your grace to spread it wildly. Grant us such unity with you and one another that you might start many new fires in the hearts of others who are drawn to our witness.

We yearn to be a movement again. We hunger for greater fruitfulness. We thirst for vitality. We cry out to be your agents of healing and life in the world. May it be so, for Christ's sake and for His glory.

Blake Busick

Pray that God would multiply our fire, faith and fruitfulness so that faith communities might become movements of God's mission in the world.

Contributors

(in order of appearance)

1. The Rev. Blake Busick, pastor, Good Samaritan UMC, Cupertino, CA and member of the Conference Vital Congregations Task Group
2. The Rev. Jerry Smith, District Superintendent, Great Northern District of the CA-NV Annual Conference
3. Cate Monaghan, Director of Communications, CA-NV Annual ConferenceThe Rev. The Rev. Sung-ho Lee, pastor, Concord UMC, Concord, CA and member of the Conference Vital Congregations Task Group
4. The Rev. Kristie Olah, District Superintendent, Camino Real District of the CA-NV Annual Conference
5. Diane Knudsen, Treasurer and Director of Administrative Services, CA-NV Annual Conference
6. The Rev. Ted Virts, Conference Superintendent
7. The Rev. Mariellen Yoshino, District Superintendent, Central Valley District of the CA-NV Annual Conference
8. Kelly Newell, Director of Camping and Young People's Ministries, CA-NV Annual Conference
9. Linda Caldwell, Conference Superintendent for Mission Collaboration
10. The Rev. Renae Extrum-Fernandez, District Superintendent, Bridges District of the CA-NV Annual Conference
11. Phil Bandy, Interim Director, United Methodist Volunteers in Mission, CA-NV Annual Conference
12. The Rev. Laurie McHugh, Associate Pastor, First UMC of Palo Alto, Palo Alto, CA
13. The Rev. George Bennett, Fulltime Local Pastor, Sanger UMC, Sanger CA and member of the Conference Vital Congregations Task Group
14. The Rev. Siosifa Hingano, pastor, Genesis UMC, San Jose, CA and Chair of the Order of Elders
15. The Rev. Mark Bollwinkel, pastor, Los Altos UMC, Los Altos, CA
16. Gayle Shearman, co-Lay Leader for the CA-NV Annual Conference

Small Group Template

May this outline provide fuel that helps your small group *Catch Fire in 50 Days.*

Welcoming (10 min)
- Make sure everyone is welcome and knows each other. Do introductions as needed.
- Use an icebreaker question (something very easy to answer and non-threatening).

Opening Prayer (2 min)
- Offer a simple prayer asking the Holy Spirit to guide your time together.
- Keep it simple so that others might be willing to do it in the future.

Singing (5 min)
- You or someone in your group might lead this.
- You could also listen to some worship music from time to time.

Sharing your faith—in groups of three (10 min)
- *How have you experienced God recently in your life?*
- The power of this question comes when you ask it every time you meet. If people expect it they will start noticing God in their life more. If you do it in groups of three you can keep the time to 10 minutes.

Reflecting on the readings from the week (30 min)
- If your pastor is preaching from one of the texts from the week, read that text and then have someone prepared to summarize the sermon.
- Choose some of the "Reflect" questions from the week for the group to discuss. Or write some of your own. Or have group members come prepared to share one of the questions or passages that was particularly meaningful to them.
- Discuss what "Responses" group members have tried to make and how that went.

Serving (5 min)

- Decide on a service project that you will do together before the end of the 50 days.
- Spend time each meeting moving this forward.

Praying (10 min)

- Share joys and concerns and pray for each other.
- Pray for each faith community to join in the movement of God's mission in the world.

Eating & Fellowshipping

The *Readiness 360* measures that which drives ministry-multiplying behavior. Now in its second generation, *Readiness 360* is an even more powerful tool for helping any church effectively engage new people in its ministry. Nothing like it exists on the market. *Readiness 360* helps churches get ready, so that new initiatives take root and thrive! Whether your church is considering a second campus, a new worship service, or simply desires to reclaim its vitality, this tool will help you multiply your impact.

The cost of the *Readiness 360* includes:

- Online inventory allowing an unlimited number people to provide input
- Customized reports with ministry tips that help congregations build on their strengths toward greater ministry effectiveness
- Three layers of reporting for a variety of audiences (summary, executive and complete)

"*Readiness 360* is a valuable resource that has come at a time when churches are moving away from an expansion-focused strategy for church growth to kingdom-minded multiplication. *Readiness 360* is a tool I highly recommend for churches of all sizes and contexts!"

Gary Shockley, Executive Director, Path 1 New Church Starts

"The *Readiness 360* is the assessment and development tool we've been looking for! It is now a required step in Missouri before we help fund a multisite, mother-daughter or other new church project launched from an existing congregation."

Bob Farr, Director of The Center for Congregational Excellence and Author,
Renovate or Die: 10 Ways to Focus Your Church on Mission

"This process was extremely helpful for our leadership team and provided insights that we would have not recognized on our own."

Dwight S. Kilbourne, Senior Minister, First-Centenary UMC (Tennessee)

Learn more at www.readiness360.org or 1-866-721-0177.

READINESS 360

Multiply your impact.

CPSIA information can be obtained at www.ICGtesting.com
Printed in the USA
BVOW010238120412

287396BV00004B/1/P

9 780984 618828